THE CHURCH OF THE SERVANT

THE CHURCH OF THE SERVANT

ANTHONY T. HANSON

WIPF & STOCK · Eugene, Oregon

Wipf and Stock Publishers
199 W 8th Ave, Suite 3
Eugene, OR 97401

The Church of the Servant
By Hanson, Anthony Tyrrell
Copyright©1962 SCM
ISBN 13: 978-1-4982-9574-1
Publication date 8/5/2016
Previously published by SCM, 1962

Copyright © SCM Press 1962
First English edition 1962 by SCM Press
This Edition published by arrangement with
Hymns Ancient & Modern Ltd.

CONTENTS

Publisher's Note 7

I · *The Biblical Basis*

1 ISRAEL MY SERVANT 11
The Servant's Obedience and Witness 13
The Songs of the Suffering Servant 18
Who is the Servant? 24

2 A SERVANT OF THE JEWISH PEOPLE 28
Jesus as the Servant 29
The Vocation of Jesus 37
The Witness of the New Testament 39

3 OURSELVES AS YOUR SERVANTS 45
I Corinthians 3.18-4.13 46
II Corinthians 4.1-15 50
II Corinthans 5.14-6.10 54

4 THE AUTHORITY OF THE SERVANT 61
St Paul on Authority 61
Authority in the Gospels 65

II · *The Church's Life*

5 THE SERVANT CHURCH 71
Social Service by the Church 73
In the Welfare State 77
What Hinders Service? 82

6 THE CENTRE OF THE CHURCH ... 86
- The Laity: the Church in the World ... 86
- The Eucharist: the World in the Church ... 92
- Conclusion ... 96

7 THE EQUIPMENT OF GOD'S PEOPLE ... 98
- Away from Hierarchy ... 99
- Ministers and Ministry ... 103

8 ONE WHO HAD AUTHORITY ... 107
- In Defence of Excommunication ... 107
- Authority in Teaching ... 111

9 SERVICE AND MISSION ... 114
- St Paul and the Missionaries ... 114
- Problems in Asia and Africa ... 116
- Towards an Eastern Church ... 119

Appendix ... 112
For Further Reading ... 124
Index of Biblical References ... 126
Index of Names ... 128

PUBLISHER'S NOTE

The theme of Jesus the Servant is a key to much Christian thought nowadays. We have had enough of antiquated myth and conventional jargon; *this* theme is clear. We have had enough of religion out of touch with reality; Jesus the Servant is eminently practical. We have had enough of the Church being identified with snobbery in the West and colonialism in the East; Jesus the Servant is utterly humble. We have had enough of Christians patronising the world; Jesus the Servant comes with a towel and a cross.

When the Student Christian Movement of Great Britain and Ireland began planning a large Congress for the first days of 1963, in Bristol, this was the theme chosen by the students. Already it had emerged as the central theme in the study of the life and mission of the Church being sponsored in many countries by the World Student Christian Federation.

But what are the biblical roots? Much of the scholarly literature is written in a style which deters non-specialists. Some of it is merely hair-splitting. Dr Hanson, already the author of two notable books of biblical theology and the joint author of two biblical commentaries, was asked to give a clear summary of what is said in the two Testaments. He bases himself on the translation of the Revised Standard Version (RSV), with some reference to the New English Bible (NEB). He was also invited to suggest how the biblical doctrine is relevant to Christian life today. In this discussion he deals with the task of the ordained ministry and with the question of authority in the Church, but the non-theologian should not be dismayed: all this discussion is important to him, because all of it is intended to show how the whole Church (most of it lay) can be the Servant, as Jesus is the Servant.

Dr Hanson taught theology in the Church of South India before returning to his native Church of Ireland as Canon Theologian of St Anne's Cathedral, Belfast. He is now Professor of Theology in the University of Hull. Many will be glad that this experience has broadened his first-hand knowledge without blunting his provocative pen.

D.L.E.

I

THE BIBLICAL BASIS

I

ISRAEL MY SERVANT

IN SOUTH INDIA social distinctions are still very clearly marked. Those who do manual work will address white-collar workers and educated people in language of respect which we in the West often find strange. I remember being puzzled during my early days in India as to why the *dhobi* always referred to his customers' belongings as '*our* shirts', '*our* towels', etc. We even heard one woman missionary friend jokingly protesting to her *dhobi* against his practice of referring to her underwear as '*our* underclothes'. Later I realized that all this was only an example, odd though it seemed to us, of a different code of politeness. The correct thing for an inferior to do was to identify himself with his superior, as client to patron: the polite implication was that he was a member of the patron's household.

Much the same usage is found in the Old Testament: when those who consider themselves inferior address their superiors, they call themselves 'your servants'. The word for 'servant' in Hebrew means really 'slave', and no doubt the original implication was that the inferior is the slave of the superior. Thus in Genesis 42.13, when Joseph's brothers appear before him to buy grain, the writer of the narrative, with superb irony, makes them refer to themselves as Joseph's slaves:

We, your servants, are twelve brothers, the sons of one man in the land of Canaan.

Similarly, when Hazael, told by Elisha of the great future that lay before him, wishes to express his sense of inadequacy, he says to the prophet (II Kings 8.13):

What is your servant who is but a dog, that he should do this great thing?

Very naturally, this usage also applied to people approaching God. We find the Psalmist exclaiming (Psalm 116.16):

> O Lord, I am thy servant;
> I am thy servant, the son of thy handmaid.
> Thou hast loosed my bonds.

All Israelites were slaves of God. God, when he calls Moses in Exodus 3.12, says:

When you have brought forth the people out of Egypt you shall serve God upon this mountain.

On the other hand, it was not everybody who was called 'the servant of God'. All Israelites were called to serve God, but only a few are distinguished by the title 'my servant'. To be called 'my servant' by God was a great and exceptional honour. Abraham received it, but only after his death. In Genesis 26.24 God appears to Isaac and says:

I am with you, and will bless you and multiply your descendants for my servant Abraham's sake.

Moses also gained the title of servant: it is applied to him in a context which shows how rarely he is privileged. In Numbers 12.6-8 God says that he will appear in visions to prophets but

Not so with my servant Moses: he is entrusted with all my house. With him I speak mouth to mouth, clearly and not in dark speech; and he beholds the form of the Lord.

Some others are described as God's special servant—David for instance. Psalm 78.70-71 says:

God chose David his servant . . . to be the shepherd of Jacob his peope, of Israel his inheritance.

There is also one particular group within Israel that is called God's servants: this is, the prophets. As with Moses so with them, their being God's servants is connected with their special knowledge of God. Amos 3.7 says:

> Surely the Lord God does nothing, without revealing his secret to his servants the prophets.

All Israel was called to serve God, but only a few in any age were acknowledged by God with the title of 'my servant'. They were all men who had a special task to perform and they were all believed to know God's mind more deeply than other men did.

The Servant's Obedience and Witness

Some men can only hear God's call to service after they have been awakened by suffering. So it was with Francis of Assisi. He only began to think about serving God in any extraordinary way when his carefree career as a rich merchant's son was checked by two events in succession, an imprisonment and a serious illness. We may say the same thing about the people of Israel as a whole. Indeed, we can even trace the parallel in greater detail and say that Israel had to experience a serious illness and an imprisonment before it could awake to God's call to service. Isaiah late in the eighth century BC said of his people:

> The whole head is sick,
> and the whole heart faint.

This sickness grew worse, till it culminated in the exile of 587 BC, the imprisonment as it is called in Isaiah 42.22. As long as the Kingdom stood, Israel could only be a middle eastern kingdom, sometimes more prosperous, sometimes in great distress, but never aspiring to be anything more than one small nation, a more or less insignificant unit in middle eastern politics. Then came the violent shock of the exile, and Israel was transformed in a few weeks from a state into a group of deported persons. This was the point at which Israel's vocation as God's servant began to be proclaimed. It was only national suffering that could bring about the circumstances in which Israel's mission as the servant could be either understood or carried out.

The man who first greeted Israel as God's servant must have begun his prophetic career a good thirty years after the exile took place, so he was speaking to a people who had had a generation in which to think about the meaning of what had happened. We do not know his name: indeed all that we know about him is what we can learn from his prophecies, which comprise chapters 40-55 of the Book of Isaiah. Because his poems have been bound up with those of Isaiah the son of Amoz who lived 740-680 BC, he is usually called the Second Isaiah. His very first word to his people is one of encouragement (40.1):

> Comfort, comfort my people,
>   Says your God.
> Speak tenderly to Jerusalem.

The message of comfort is that the time of suffering is ended, and that Israel is to return to Jerusalem led by the hand of God himself. It is Cyrus, king of Media, who is to be the instrument of God's action (45.1-6). He is to overthrow Babylon, and thus open the way for Israel's return to the home land.

But in all this Israel as the Lord's servant has a special part to play. In the very same passage where Cyrus is most clearly referred to (45.4), Israel is addressed as 'Servant of the Lord'. God says to Cyrus:

> For the sake of my servant Jacob,
>   and Israel my chosen,
> I call you by your name,
>   surname you, though you do not know me.

ISRAEL MY SERVANT

Scattered through the rest of Second Isaiah's prophecy are references which further define Israel's task as the servant of the Lord. These sixteen chapters do not form a closely-knit argument, one theme leading on to another in logical sequence. They are not like a dialogue of Plato, or one of Jesus' discourses in the fourth gospel. Second Isaiah resembles all the other prophets of the Old Testament in this, that what we have of his writings is only a collection of prophecies uttered on different occasions. We cannot assume that because one verse occurs later than another it must have been written later. We quote therefore simply what we can find about the vocation of Israel as the Servant of the Lord in chapters 40-55 of Isaiah.

We find in fact that Israel's duty as the servant reduces itself to two things: Israel must *obey* and *witness*.

Here is a clear call to *obedience* (41.8-10):

> But you, Israel my servant,
>   Jacob whom I have chosen,
> The offspring of Abraham my friend;
> You whom I took from the ends of the earth,
>   and called from its farther corners,
> Saying to you, 'You are my servant,
>   I have chosen you and not cast you off',
> fear not, for I am with you.
>   be not dismayed, for I am your God;
> I will strengthen you, I will help you,
>   I will uphold you with my victorious right hand.

But Israel is not told to *do* anything here. The command is to listen. Israel is being addressed by God, Israel is one who is called. The people is to be used in the carrying out of God's purpose. Only to listen to God is to obey him. Indeed in Hebrew the verb 'to hear' (*shāma'*) frequently also means 'to obey'. We find exactly the same message in 44.1-2.

> But now hear (*shāma'*) O Jacob, my servant,
>   Israel whom I have chosen!

> Thus says the Lord, who made you,
>   who formed you from the womb and will help you:
> Fear not, O Jacob my servant
>   Jeshurun whom I have chosen.[1]

The same theme of 'hearing' is implied in 42.18-19:

> Hear, you deaf;
>   and look, you blind, that you may see!
> Who is blind but my servant,
>   or deaf as my messenger whom I send?

Here there appears the suggestion that the people are failing to respond. All God asks at the moment is attention, but even that seems beyond the mass of the people. Already we are being led beyond the simple conception of the people Israel as the Servant of the Lord. The people as a whole seems unable to respond. (See also 43.8.)

The second element in 'Israel my Servant's' duty is *witness*. This is a more active office: the people are to respond to God's call by noting what he tells them of his purpose and then, when the purpose is carried out, witnessing that he had foretold it. This is what God says in 43.10-12:

> You are my witnesses, says the Lord,
>   And my servant whom I have chosen,
> that you may know and believe me
>   and understand that I am he. . . .
> I, I am the Lord,
>   and beside me there is no saviour.
> I declared and saved and proclaimed,
>   when there was no strange God among you;
> and you are my witnesses, says the Lord.

This is not a very clear passage, as the servant seems to be distinguished from the people. But the call to witness stands out

---

[1] *Jeshurun* seems to be a sort of 'pet-name' for the people, connected with the root *jashar*. It should mean 'the upright one'. Here perhaps it is used in contrast to Jacob, which means literally 'the crooked one'.

clearly and they seem to be called to witness in time to come that God has brought about the mighty work which he is about to do. This is confirmed by verses 19-21 of the same chapter:

> Behold, I am doing a new thing,
>   now it springs forth, do you not perceive it?
> I will make a way in the wilderness
>   and rivers in the desert ...
> to give drink to my chosen people,
>   the people whom I formed for myself,
> that they might declare my praise.

God is about to create a road across the desert, by which his people can return to the homeland; and they must respond by declaring his praise. They are to witness to God's mighty acts and now they are being called to prepare themselves. And here is another passage in which singular and plural nouns occur in lines where the meaning is parallel, suggesting that Israel as a whole is still thought of as capable of responding to God's call (44.24-26):

> Thus says the Lord, your Redeemer,
>   who formed you from the womb:
> I am the Lord, who made all things,
>   who stretched out the heavens above ...
> who confirms the word of his servant,
>   and performs the counsel of his messengers:
> who says of Jerusalem: She shall be inhabited,
>   and of the cities of Judah: They shall be built.

If Israel responds to God's call, they will rise up as one man, proclaim the coming deliverance, and follow God's leading back to their ruined homes in Judah.

Other passages could be quoted: 44.8, 21; 48.6; and perhaps the obscure pasasge 55.3-5. But we will be content with one more, where the thought of witness to prophecy fulfilled is very clear. It is 44.7-8:

> Who has announced from of old the things to come?
>   Let them tell us what is yet to be.
> Fear not, nor be afraid:
>   have I not told you from of old and declared it?
> And you are my witnesses!

The people as a whole are called to listen to God as he declares his purpose for the immediate future, in order that, when it comes to pass, they may be able to witness to prophecy fulfilled and to the mighty acts of God.

The Songs of the Suffering Servant

There still remain to be mentioned four important passages in which the Servant's mission is set forth in greater detail than anywhere else. But their relation to the rest of the prophecy of the Second Isaiah is not very simple or obvious. Perhaps an analogy from ancient Greek literature may be the best way of approaching this part of the Book. Not quite a hundred and fifty years after the Second Isaiah spoke his words to Israel in exile, drama in Athens reached its climax with the plays of Aeschylus and Sophocles and Euripides. In these plays there is one feature which gives us a remote analogy to a feature in our prophet's work, and that is the use of the lyrics uttered by the chorus. In all three dramatists (except for the very earliest work of Aeschylus) the action of the play is conveyed in the iambic metre which coresponds fairly well to English blank verse; but at intervals the regular iambic metre is interrupted by lyrics in a great variety of metres sung by the chorus. These lyrical interludes serve a double purpose: they give an opportunity for reflecting on the significance of what is happening, and they heighten the particular emotional tone which the dramatist wishes to convey. For example, in Sophocles' play *Antigone* there is a famous lyric beginning with the words: 'There are many wonderful things, but none of them is more wonderful than man.' In it Sophocles considers the astonishing nature of *homo sapiens*, his amazing skill and equally amazing weakness. So also in the *Agamemnon* of Aeschylus one lyrical interlude begins: 'Why does this fear stand like a steady sentinel by my foreboding mind?' It goes on to increase the feeling of dread and foreboding, which the dramatist uses as a preparation for the murder of Agamemnon. We may look on these choric interludes as passages in which the emotional tone of the play is intensified, and the true significance of the action emphasized.

A modern parallel can be traced in T. S. Eliot's *Four Quartets*. In each of the four parts of this long poem we find a short lyrical passage in which the emotional tone of the poem is heightened. In two of these at least, the lyric serves also to elucidate the meaning of the poem as a whole by means of an analogy or symbol. Thus in *East Coker*, the lyric beginning 'The wounded surgeon plies the steel' gives us the image of the world as a hospital, and in *Little Gidding* the lovely lyric beginning 'The dove descending breaks the air . . .' has in the figure of the incendiary bomb a symbol of judgment and mercy.

These two parallels from other literature should help us to approach what are called the Servant Songs in the prophecies of the Second Isaiah. Up to this point we have only been considering those passages in his work where Israel as a whole is clearly thought of as the Servant of the Lord; but now we must take into account the four Servant Songs, where the identity of the Servant is not so clear. These four Songs have been isolated by scholars because they are in certain respects different from the rest of chapters 40-55. They are as follows:

        42. 1-4: the first Song
        49. 1-6: the second Song
        50. 4-9: the third Song
        52. 13-53. 12: the fourth Song.

Scholars are agreed on the distinctive character of these Songs, but there is no agreement as to their relation to the rest of Second Isaiah's prophecies. Till recently many scholars held the view that they were written by someone else, a disciple perhaps; but today the tendency is to deny this. Nor can we be at all certain they there were written exactly in the context in which they appear; in fact, for instance, many scholars hold that the fourth Song is the latest of the prophet's utterances. What we can say is this: in these four Servant Songs we find the two elements which we saw in the lyrics in Greek drama and in T. S. Eliot. The emotional tone is intensified, and the significance of the Servant's mission is profoundly expressed. In the course of this, the prophet's whole conception of the Servant seems to have undergone a development. That is why we must give the Songs special attention.

The first Servant Song (42.1-4) is fairly straightforward. Verse 1 shows that the Servant is the instrument of God's purpose:

> I have put my spirit upon him.

In verse 4, the Servant's aim is described thus:

> till he has established justice in the earth;
> and the coastlands wait for his law.

Many scholars would prefer to translate that word 'justice' as 'religion' and 'law' as 'instruction'. The verse refers to the world mission of Israel to spread the religion of the Lord to all peoples. Indeed, this Song would seem to think of the whole nation as the Servant, except for verses 2-3:

> He will not cry or lift up his voice,
> or make it heard in the street;
> a bruised reed he will not break
> and a dimly burning wick he will not quench.

This suggests a ministry of quiet persuasion: could a whole

nation carry out such a ministry? We are left with a question in our minds.

The second Servant Song (49.1-6) brings this question sharply to the forefront. In verses 1-4 the Servant speaks and seems to be Israel as a whole; but in verses 6-9 the Servant is given a mission both to his own people and to the world.

> It is too light a thing that you should be my servant
> to raise up the tribes of Jacob
> and to restore the preserved of Israel;
> I will give you as a light to the nations,
> that my salvation may reach to the end of the earth.

Here for the first time the conception of the whole of Israel as the Servant breaks down: the Servant is called to bring the exiled back; therefore the Servant cannot be defined simply as the people Israel. We are driven to assume that only some part of Israel has responded to the prophet's call, and it is to this responsive group that his word is addressed. How do we reconcile this with verse 3?

> You are my servant,
> Israel in whom I will be glorified.

Many scholars have fallen to the temptation simply to cut out the word 'Israel' here: a later scribe's mistaken comment, they have said. But this is not necessary; even though only one group within Israel has responded to the call of God, their mission is still Israel's mission. The obedient remnant acts on behalf of the disobedient whole: this is a truth which we shall find of great significance later.

The third Servant Song (50.4-9) leads us perhaps a little further: we hear for the first time of the sufferings of the Servant. Here nothing worse seems indicated than contempt and rejection:

> I gave my back to the smiters,
> and my cheeks to those who pulled out the beard;

> I hid not my face
> from shame and spitting.

The Servant seems to be even more definitely associated with the faithful group here; if we compare verse 4, where the Servant is surely thought of as encouraging his own people, with the experience described in verse 6, we have the impression that the Servant represents a missionary group or even perhaps is himself an individual with a mission. This prepares us for *the fourth Song* (52.13-53.12).

This is the longest and also the most obscure of the Servant Songs. In some places (e.g. 53.10) the original meaning of the Hebrew is not by any means certain. It is not even clear who is speaking throughout the Song. For example, who is the 'we' of 53.1-6? Is it the rest of Israel? Or the faithful group? Or the Prophet? Or the Gentiles? Also, the wide range of meaning conveyed by the Hebrew imperfect tense adds a further element of uncertainty. Especially in 53.7-12, it is uncertain whether the imperfect tense refers to present or future; and in poetry the other tense, the perfect, does not necessarily always denote action in the past! Thus it is quite possible for scholars to maintain that the whole action described in the last Servant Song is still in the future from the point of view of the prophet.

However, we can distinguish four important features in the picture of the Servant presented here. First of all, it is almost impossible to imagine that the prophet did not have an individual in mind: this comes out specially clearly in 52.14-53.3.

> His appearance was so marred, beyond human semblance, and his form beyond that of the sons of men . . . he had no form or comeliness that we should look at him, and no beauty that we should desire him . . . a man of sorrows and acquainted with grief.[1]

[1] It is quite possible that the real meaning is: 'a man of pains and acquainted with sickness'.

ISRAEL MY SERVANT

This is not language that can be used of a group: it must denote some individual. Secondly, the Servant by his sufferings has brought atonement for the sin of others. Indeed, he seems to be a substitute for sinners, in the sense that he received the punishment that was their due. Moreover, this is God's deliberate will (53.5-6).

> But he was wounded for our transgressions,
>   he was bruised for our iniquities;
> upon him was the chastisement that made us whole,
>   and with his stripes we are healed. . . .
> The Lord has laid upon him
>   the iniquity of us all.

The prophet makes no attempt to explain how this atoning work can have been accomplished, nor does he ask any questions about the justice of God. It is God's work, carried out through the Servant. The next point is closely connected with this one: the Servant voluntarily accepted an unjust death. This is the detail outlined in 53.7-9. It is an obscure passage, but the main outlines stand out: he was unjustly condemned and put to death; he was actually buried. He made no protest against this, though he was completely innocent. The Servant is not represented as actively going out to meet this unjust fate. His part is a passive one:

> like a lamb that is led to the slaughter.

But we are not to think of the Servant as the mere puppet of the divine will:

> he bore the sin of many,
>   and made intercession for the transgressors.

These last words of 53.12 do suggest an active acceptance of his rôle of innocent sufferer. Finally, somewhere, somehow, the Servant is to be vindicated and is to survive death. This is described in 53.10-12, the most obscure passage in all the prophecy of the Second Isaiah, so we cannot be certain about details. But, if these verses do not describe the vindication of the Servant after death, they have no meaning at all.

Who is the Servant?

It is not surprising that many people since New Testament times have echoed the question which the Ethiopian eunuch put to Philip in Acts 8.34:

> About whom, pray, does the prophet say this,
> about himself, or about someone else?

The obvious answer which occurs at once to the minds of Christians is 'Jesus Christ', the answer which in fact Philip did give. It is, we must confess, the only ultimately satisfactory answer, but we must make quite plain that put abruptly in this way, it just cannot stand. We cannot say, for instance, that the prophet, as he wrote these words, was consciously thinking of a certain Jesus of Nazareth to be born more than 500 years later. Apart from any other considerations, not every little detail of the fourth Servant Song fits Jesus of Nazareth. He was not, as far as we know, a man of unattractive (far less inhuman) appearance. His grave was not with the wicked. Again, to suggest that Second Isaiah consciously foresaw Jesus of Nazareth is to misunderstand the nature of Old Testament prophecy. The prophet's first task was to declare God's will for his own situation. If the prophet was thinking *only* of Jesus as he wrote this Song, then he was saying something that had no immediate reference; it would only begin to be relevant 500 years later.

The immediate question, therefore, remains: of whom was the prophet speaking? As far as the material outside the Servant Songs is concerned the answer must be: the people Israel. But in the Songs themselves that answer has been shown to be inadequate: at times the prophet seems to be thinking of the faithful group in Israel, the people who would listen and obey. But ultimately (and especially in the last Song) even the faithful group fails to fit the picture: he must be thinking of some individual.

Who is this individual? As we read the last Song over, some of the great figures in Israel's history seem to appear for a moment in the background of the picture. *Moses,* we know, was willing to offer his life, innocent though he was, for his sinful people in the wilderness. We remember Exodus 32.32:

But now, if thou wilt, forgive their sin—and if not blot me, I pray thee, out of thy book.

Isaiah whom God calls 'my servant' in Isaiah 20.3, met with scorn and rejection (Isaiah 28.9), and there is a tradition (perhaps referred to in Hebrews 11.37) that he was put to death by King Manasseh. *Jeremiah* refers to himself thus (11.19):

But I was like a gentle lamb led to the slaughter.

And if ever any man deserved the description 'a man of sorrows, and acquainted with grief' it was he. *Jehoiachin,* regarded by many Jews as the last legitimate king to sit on the throne of David, was unjustly condemned and imprisoned. We even learn of his vindication at the end of his life (see II Kings 25.27-30).

All these historical persons seem to have something in common with the Servant of the Lord in Second Isaiah, but none completely fills the picture. We cannot doubt that their experiences have contributed some details to the figure of the Servant; but it has proved impossible to say of any one of them 'the prophet must have been thinking of him and him alone'. It is not surprising that today probably the majority of scholars would agree that the individual described in the fourth Servant Song had not yet appeared when the prophet wrote. The Servant who gives his life for Israel and for the Gentiles was

Israel, but Israel represented by an individual who was still to come.

At the end we are left with a mystery: Israel has been called to be the Servant of the Lord. Israel as a whole fails to respond to the call, though there is no doubt a faithful group in Israel who hear in the prophet's words the call of God. But by the end of his ministry, disappointed perhaps by the failure of Cyrus to acknowledge the God of whom he is the unconscious instrument, Second Isaiah sees the mission of the Servant deepening and widening: he is to recall all, Gentiles as well as Jews, to the worship of the only true God; and the means by which he is to bring them back from the paths in which they are straying is the voluntary sacrifice of his own life. For such a task no group, however obedient, was adequate; it had to be some one dedicated individual, who would sum up in himself the obedience and self-sacrifice of all the heroes of Israel's history. Such an individual had not yet appeared; but when he does appear he will sum up in himself the full meaning of 'Israel my Servant'.

It is not a choice of *either* Israel the nation *or* the individual Israelite: the Servant of the Lord, when he appears, is to be Israel in himself, the fountain and the representative of the new obedient Israel, the Israel that had never yet existed, but the Israel as God meant it to be, the perfectly obedient Servant.

Our great concern, finally, in studying the prophecy of Second Isaiah is to understand what light it throws on Jesus Christ, his conception of his own vocation, and the account of him which his first disciples gave. What is *most* important for us, therefore, is not what the Second Isaiah meant by his prophecies (though we cannot ignore the light thrown by this), but what those prophecies meant to Jesus and to his first disciples.

It is quite certain that Jesus and the men who wrote about

him in the New Testament did not think in terms of First and Second Isaiah, or of four Servant Songs. They saw the Book of Isaiah as a whole and they received its message as a whole. Jesus, we may be sure, did not see any break at chapter 39 or again at chapter 55. He read the Book straight through. He must have found there a message about the Servant of the Lord, a Servant who was sometimes explicitly identified with the people Israel, but at other times was quite clearly some one individual. This Servant, he would understand, was called to a great mission, and the mission comprised three things: he must obey, he must witness, and he must suffer. By so doing he would be carrying out God's redemptive purpose for Israel and for the world.

2

A SERVANT OF THE JEWISH PEOPLE

IF THERE is one verse in the gospels that has caused more heart-searching to commentators than any other, it is Mark 13.32, where Jesus says that not even the Son knows the hour of his coming in glory. The difficulty has always been that it seems to imply a limitation of knowledge on Jesus' part. Cyril of Alexandria (who died in AD 444) was reduced to saying: 'He pretended not to know, for the benefit of his hearers.' Up till the last century most scholars thought they were bound to defend Jesus' omniscience as a proof and sign of his divinity. But today most theologians would insist on just the opposite. The fact that his knowledge was limited, and that he thought and spoke in the terms of his own day is itself a proof of the wonderful humility of God. Incarnation must imply limitation. But this conclusion brings up at once the question: what were the terms in which Jesus thought? And in particular: in what terms did Jesus think about himself? In what light did he see his own vocation? Once we have given up the conception of an all-knowing Jesus, carrying out a scheme of salvation which he had learned in heaven, we are at once faced with the urgent question: in what sense was he conscious of being God? Thus the question of Jesus' consciousness of his own vocation is one which we can neither take as answered, nor ignore.

There is far too much to say for us to be able to give a full consideration of it here. Most theologians in framing an answer would certainly refer to the two titles Messiah and Son of

Man. Jesus did see himself as called to be Messiah and Son of Man (in whatever sense he gave to those words). But was there a third part also which be believed himself to be fulfilling? Did he also see his vocation in terms of the Servant of the Lord in Second Isaiah?

Jesus as the Servant

Jesus began his ministry by proclaiming a message. This is clearly expressed in Mark 1.14-15:

Now after John was arrested, Jesus came into Galilee, preaching the gospel of God, and saying: 'The time is fulfilled, and the Kingdom of God is at hand; repent and believe in the gospel.'

The same words are echoed in the first and third gospels.[1] The gospel proclaimed by Jesus was the message that God's decisive act of redemption was about to take place. As we read on in St Mark's gospel, we realize that that act is intimately connected with the life and death of Jesus himself. But this very proclamation has the prophecy of Second Isaiah as its background. At several points in his prophecy, Second Isaiah refers to one who is to proclaim the message of God's deliverance. The first such passage is Isaiah 40.9:

> Get you up to a high mountain,
> O Zion, herald of good tidings,
> Lift up your voice with strength,
> O Jerusalem, herald of good tidings.

The RSV margin here offers an alternative translation: 'O herald of good tidings to Zion', and similarly in the fourth line. That this was the original meaning is confirmed by 52.7:

> How beautiful upon the mountains are the feet of him
> who brings good tidings . . .
> who publishes salvation,
> who says to Zion, 'Your God reigns'.

[1] In all the quotations from the first three gospels in this chapter, passages in Matthew and Luke that are mere reproductions of passages in Mark are not treated as evidence in addition to the Markan passage in question.

We can trace a direct verbal link between Mark 1.14-15 and these passages, for the word for 'gospel' in Mark, *euangelion*, comes from the same root as the word used by the Greek translators of Second Isaiah's Hebrew to render 'herald of good tidings' in 40.9 and 'who brings good tidings' in 52.7. The Hebrew verb comes from the root *basar*; and we find exactly the same verbal correspondences in 60.6 and 61.1. This last passage is of special significance, because, according to St Luke, this is the passage that Jesus quoted in his sermon in the synagogue at Nazareth. Luke 4.17-18 tells us that Jesus read the following words from Isaiah (61.1):

> The Spirit of the Lord is upon me,
>   because he has anointed me to *preach good news* to the poor.

The words we have put in italics are rendered by the *euangelion* root in Greek and the *basar* root in Hebrew. And here is Jesus directly claiming to be the Spirit-anointed messenger of God.[1]

It is clear that Jesus identified himself with the 'herald of good tidings' of Second Isaiah. In the time of the exile the task of that herald was to announce the good news of God's approaching act of deliverance for his people. So Jesus also announced the good news of the coming of the Kingdom of God, and in so doing identified himself with God's purpose as foreshadowed in Second Isaiah's prophecy.

We might put with this the reference to Second Isaiah which some scholars trace in Mark 14.24. Jesus, in instituting the Lord's Supper, says, as he gives the cup to his disciples:

This is my blood of the covenant, which is poured out for many.

[1] Nearly all scholars believe that Iaiah 56-66 came from a later period than the exile, but this is irrelevant to the question that concerns us. By the time of Jesus the Book was complete, and Jesus would see all of the Book of Isaiah as a unity.

A SERVANT OF THE JEWISH PEOPLE

'The blood of the covenant' has no doubt reference to other Old Testament passages as well, but it does not seem irrelevant to refer to Isaiah 42.6, where God says about the Servant:

I have given you as a covenant to the people, a light to the nations.

Once more, we see Jesus identifying himself with God's purpose as disclosed in the prophecy of Second Isaiah.

This last reference would seem to point directly towards the figure of the Servant of Second Isaiah. Now there are two passages in the first three gospels where Jesus describes himself as a servant. As we look at them, we may be able to decide whether this means that he thought of himself as *the* Servant.

The first and greatest passage is Mark 10.43-45:

Whoever would be great among you must be your servant, and whoever would be first among you must be slave of all. For the Son of Man also came not to be served, but to serve, and to give his life as a ransom for many.

The two Greek words in verses 43 and 44 are *diakonos* and *doulos* respectively, and the word for 'serve' in verse 45 is connected with the root *diakonos*. These Greek words do not link up directly with the Greek translation for 'servant' in Second Isaiah, but it is very difficult to imagine where Jesus derived the thought of service from, if not from the Second Isaiah chapters. Even if he was thinking chiefly of passages in other Old Testament books where, for example, the prophets are described as God's servants, the Hebrew word for 'servant' in such passages could only be *'ebed,* the same word as is used for the Servant of the Lord throughout Isaiah. Again, Jesus goes on to describe the sort of service he has come to do as finding its climax when he gives his life 'as a ransom for many'; and here many scholars have thought there is a direct echo of Isaiah 53. The Greek word for ransom (*lutron*) does not occur in the Greek translation of Isaiah 40-66, but the verb connected with it, 'to ransom', does frequently. No fewer than eleven times in these chapters does God speak of 'ransoming' his people.[1] We have already seen that Jesus identified himself with God's redeeming purpose as proclaimed by Second Isaiah. It does not seem at all absurd to suggest that in the saying recorded in Mark 10.43-45 Jesus had some such passage as this in mind from Isaiah 53.5:

> But he was wounded for our transgressions,
>   he was bruised for our iniquities.

Or this (53.12):

> He poured out his soul to death,
>   and was numbered with the transgressors;
> yet he bore the sin of many,
>   and made intercession for the transgressors.

This last passage is actually quoted by Jesus, according to Luke 22.37, at the time of his arrest. Some scholars would dismiss this as being Luke's interpretative addition, but it fits in very well with Jesus' whole ministry. He was accused of consorting with publicans and sinners. If Luke was interpreting Jesus' action here, he was interpreting it rightly.

Luke records another saying in which Jesus claims a servant's status for himself, Luke 22.27:

For which is the greater, one who sits at table, or one who serves? Is it not the one who sits at table? But I am among you as one who serves.

This confirms the teaching recorded in Mark 10.45, and points us back again to the Servant of Second Isaiah. It is true of course that the Servant of the Lord is Isaiah is always described as serving God, and not as serving others. But we have seen that the supreme example of service which Jesus gives consists in his giving of his life for others, and this thought is the

[1] This includes Isaiah 35.9, a chapter which there is some reason to believe belongs to the section 40-55.

central theme of the fourth Servant Song. It seems therefore unduly sceptical to look, as some have done, for the inspiration behind the saying recorded in Luke 22.27 anywhere else than in Isaiah 53.

Two more possible references to the Servant of Second Isaiah lie in what Jesus says about himself, of which the first is Mark 9.12. After the Transfiguration on the mount, the disciples ask Jesus about the coming of Elijah, which was expected before the Messiah came. He answers:

Elijah does come first to restore all things, and how is it written of the Son of Man, that he should suffer many things and be treated with contempt?

The Greek word for 'be treated with contempt' is the same as that used in one ancient Greek translation of the Hebrew of Isaiah 53.3:

He was despised, and we esteemed him not.

Indeed it is difficult to imagine to what other passage in the Old Testament the words 'it is written' in Mark 9.12 could refer.

The other passage is Luke 11.21-22, Jesus' answer to the accusation that he used Satanic power to cast out demons:

When a strong man, fully armed, guards his own palace, his goods are in peace; but when one stronger than he assails him and overcomes him, he take away his armour in which he trusted and divides his spoil.

This could be a reference to Isaiah 53.12:

Therefore I will divide him a portion with the great,
and he shall divide the spoil with the strong.

The Servant by his voluntary death is to conquer. Compare also Isaiah 49.24-25.

Linked with these references to himself as a servant we find several passages in which Jesus strongly emphasizes that his disciples must be prepared to be servants also. The most important passage we have so far studied, Mark 10.43-45, bears clear witness to this.[1] Equally clear is Mark 9.33-37. Jesus finds that the disciples have been discussing the exciting question' 'Who is the greatest?' He calls the Twelve and says:

If anyone would be first, he must be last of all and servant (*diakonos*) of all.

This is also the teaching of Luke 14.7-11, where we have the command to seek the least honourable place at table. And we can also cite Matthew 23.10-12:

Neither be called masters, for you have one master, the Christ. He who is greatest among you shall be your servant.

Indeed this last sentence could well be quoted as additional evidence of Jesus' vocation to be a servant, for 'he that is greatest among you' can only refer to Jesus himself. This emphasis on humility, supremely shown in the Master, and to be reflected in the disciples, is of absolutely central importance in Jesus' conception of his own vocation. Wherever the inspiration for this came from, it is something with which we must reckon when we come to work out the implications of Jesus' life, death and resurrection for the character of the Church. When we do try to trace its roots in the Old Testament, it is impossible to ignore the significance of the Servant of the Lord of Second Isaiah.

Perhaps most important of all in Jesus' conception of his own vocation was the conviction that he must suffer and die. This conviction is dramatically disclosed in Mark's narrative just after Peter's great recognition of Jesus as the Messiah in Mark 8.27-30. The very next verse runs:

And he began to teach them that the Son of Man must suffer

[1] And so does Luke 22.25-27, already discussed.

many things, and be rejected by the elders and the chief priests and the scribes, and be killed, and after three days rise again.

After this first reference to his death in Mark's gospel, Jesus frequently brings up the subject. In 9.30-31 and 10.32-34 we have two more explicit references to his approaching death. The actual details of scourging, spitting and crucifixion may not have been foretold with such accuracy by Jesus himself; they may be partly Mark's reconstruction of what he said, in the light of actual events. But few will attempt to deny that Jesus believed he must suffer and die. That death had a purpose, or rather it was part of God's purpose: this is made clear by the three references to his death being connected with the fulfilment of Scripture which we find in Mark 14.21, 27, 49. The same impression is given by Mark 10.38, where Jesus speaks of his approaching death as a cup to be drunk and a baptism to be undergone. It is not fanciful to point out that these two figures correspond to the two great gospel sacraments, and that in both the sacraments we recognize the meaning of Christ's death. We find an independent reference to the same thought in Luke 12.50:

I have a baptism to be baptised with; and how I am constrained until it is accomplished.

Jesus believed that his death was necessary, and that by it God's purpose for his people would be carried out.

But why was it necessary for him to suffer and die? What made him so certain that the Son of man must die?

In a general sense it was partly no doubt that he saw himself as the last of a long line of prophets, many of whom had been rejected and some put to death by the Jews of old. This strain comes out clearly in Luke 13.32-34:

Behold I cast out demons and perform cures today and tomorrow, and the third day I finish my course. Nevertheless I must go on my way today and tomorrow and the day following, for it cannot be that a prophet should perish away from Jerusalem. O Jerusalem, Jerusalem, killing the prophets and stoning those who are sent to you! How often would I have gathered your children together as a hen gathers her brood under her wings, and you would not!

The same belief is witnessed to (apparently independently) in the long and terrible denunciation of the scribes and Pharisees in Matthew 23, which ends with the words (23.35):

. . . that upon you may come all the righteous blood shed on earth from the blood of innocent Abel to the blood of Zechariah the son of Barachiah, whom you murdered between the sanctuary and the altar.

Here is an interpretation of Israel's history according to which God's people has always been disobedient and rebellious: their alienation from God, it is clearly implied, is to reach its climax in the murder of the Messiah himself.

This element in Jesus' teaching brings us right back to the suffering Servant in Second Isaiah. We have seen how Israel the Servant is first of all called to listen to God speaking through his prophet, and to obey. We have seen how the prophet's experience of rejection leads him on to think of a faithful group who will accept the burden of the Servant's mission, and how the prophet eventually came to the conclusion that it could only be one perfectly obedient individual who by his voluntary suffering and death could adequately carry out Israel's task as the Servant. In Isaiah 53.11 that individual is called 'the righteous one, my servant'. The significance of 'all the righteous blood shed upon earth' is summed up and expressed in the death of the Servant in just the way that the rejection and suffering of all the prophets is summed up and brought to fruition in the suffering and death of Jesus. The prophets were God's servants if anyone was, and in the death of Jesus the meaning of the deaths of both the Servant and the servants is finally understood.

The Vocation of Jesus

Did Jesus see himself as the Servant? The question implies that for Jesus there was a certain figure to be traced in Isaiah 40-55, and to be clearly distinguished from what went before and after in Israel's sacred literature. In this sense we may be sure that Jesus did not consciously identify himself with the Servant, for he did not look at Scripture in that way. For him there were no textual problems; there was only what he read about Israel's mission in the Book of the prophet Isaiah. But what is to be found there does tally in the most remarkable way with the actual pattern of Jesus' life, the aims which, as far as we can judge from the records, he set before himself.

We have claimed that the Servant of the Lord, whether people or individual, had three duties laid upon him: the duty of *obedience,* the duty of *witness,* and the duty of *suffering.* All these three are prominent themes in Jesus' life. His *obedience* to the Father is underlined first in the voice at his baptism in Mark 1.11:

> Thou art my beloved Son; with thee I am well pleased.[1]

This obedience is at once tested and demonstrated in the temtation which follows; and it reaches its climax at Gethsemane, where Jesus finally accepts the destiny of the Cross with the words (Mark 14.36):

> not what I will, but what thou wilt.

Jesus' ministry of *witness* is shown very early in Mark's gospel when he comes preaching the gospel of God's impending redemption. It is well summed up in John 18.37:

[1] It is significant that several scholars see in this sentence an echo of Isaiah 42.1.

> For this I was born, and for this I have come into the world, to bear witness to the truth.

Jesus' message was part of his vocation, and it corresponds very closely with the message of Second Isaiah. When Jesus says in the synagogue at Nazareth (Luke 4.21):

> Today this scripture has been fulfilled in your hearing,

he is doing exactly what the Servant in Isaiah was called out to do in the days of the coming deliverance: he is witnessing to the fulfilment of scripture in the act of God's redemption. And it is hardly necessary to stress the third duty, *suffering*. We have seen how integral to his vocation this was in Jesus' thought about himself.

To obey, to witness, to suffer: this was the duty of the Servant, and also the vocation of Jesus. But in Second Isaiah it was also the destiny of Israel. And we can take a further step: Jesus saw himself as the heir of Israel's destiny. This is made clearest of all in the parable of the Wicked Husbandmen as narrated in Mark 12.1-11. That parable is itself based on the Song of the Vineyard in Isaiah 5.1-7. Isaiah describes Israel under the figure of a vineyard: God had planted it and tended it but it only brought forth sour grapes in the end; so he will leave it to run wild. In Jesus' parable the vineyard and the tenants together represent Old Israel; God sends to them a succession of servants; these must represent the prophets and righteous men whose blood has been shed in the past by disobedient Israel. Finally he sends his Son, and him the tenants put to death. Because of this the vineyard will be given to others. Once again the destiny of the servants has culminated in the destiny of Jesus. The new Israel that is to be born begins in him.

In the deepest sense, therefore, Jesus did see himself as the Servant of the Lord and also the servant of the Jewish people.

But this did not mean that he separated himself from Israel. Just as the Servant in Second Isaiah is both the people Israel and the individual who represents Israel's true mission, so Jesus is both the Servant-Messiah rejected by disobedient and blind Israel, and also in himself the heir to Israel's destiny, who carried out in his own person the obedient service God requires from Israel. The destiny of Israel as a whole is reflected in the destiny of God's faithful servants throughout Israel's history; and the destiny of the servants of the Lord is supremely expressed in the destiny of the one Servant who gave his life as a ransom for many. What we know of Jesus' conception of his own vocation is coloured by the picture of the Suffering Servant, but in order to understand it better, we must set it in the context of the whole history of the people of Israel.

The Witness of the New Testament

On the evidence of the first three gospels, Jesus thought of himself as the Servant of the Lord. All St Paul's epistles were written before the earliest of the gospels, and while we should not expect them to give us light on Jesus' conception of his vocation, they do give us valuable insight into what it meant to the early Church to say that Jesus is the Servant-Messiah.

In one very important passage St Paul describes Jesus as taking the status of a slave. It is the famous incarnation passage in Philippians (2.6-7):

> who, though he was in the form of God, did not count equality with God a thing to be grasped, but emptied himself taking the form of a servant, being born in the likeness of men.

The phrase 'emptied himself' is a strange one. It has been pointed out that it is an exact translation of the Hebrew phrase in Isaiah 53.12 which the RSV renders:

> he poured out his soul to death.

The Hebrew word for 'poured out' is literally 'made bare' and of course 'his soul' is the regular Hebrew idiom for the reflexive pronoun, himself. The use of this phrase in conjunction with the word 'servant' (*doulos,* literally a 'slave'), points very clearly to Isaiah 53. In fact, there is here a remarkable possibility. Scholars suggest that this great hymn of the incarnation which we find in Philippians 2.5-11 is not Paul's free composition, but that he is quoting a formula already known to the Philippians, a liturgical hymn or creed. If this is so, then the conception of Jesus as the Servant (with special connection with the Servant in Second Isaiah) can be traced very far back indeed.[1]

In one place where Paul describes Christ as a servant, he uses the other Greek word, diakonos. The passage is Romans 15.7-12:

Welcome one another, therefore, as Christ has welcomed you, for the glory of God. For I tell you that Christ became a servant to the circumcised to shew God's truthfulness, in order to confirm the promises given to the patriarchs, and in order that the Gentiles might glorify God for his mercy.

Then in verses 9-12 he goes on to quote a number of Old Testament passages in order to show that Christ was destined to gather the Jews and Gentiles together in the worship of the true God.

Perhaps the New English Bible translation brings out the meaning even more clearly:

> Christ became a servant of the Jewish people.

The thought behind this is startling in its simplicity. Christ came as a Servant to his own people in order to fulfil God's

[1] Some supporting evidence for this idea may be found in the fact that 'he emptied himself' seems to be a direct translation (independent of the official Greek translation called the Septuagint) of a phrase in Isaiah 53. Only the very first Christians, who were all Jews, would have been competent to translate *directly* from the Hebrew into Greek.

age-old promises. God had always intended that Israel should receive their Messiah, and that the Gentiles also should come to worship God through the Messiah. The way this purpose was to be achieved was by the Messiah becoming a Servant. This passage bears a remarkable resemblance in form and content to Philippians 2.1-11. In both passages the aim is to encourage Christians to mutual love and help by the example of Christ's entering into fellowship with us; in both the theme of incarnation is central; in both Christ's humiliation is prominent; in both Christ is pictured as speaking in the words of the Old Testament (see Philippians 2.10-11 and Isaiah 45.23). In both the glory of the Father is the ultimate end.[1] Quite plainly, therefore, Christ's being a Servant was an essential part of his redemptive action in St Paul's view, and this view was not peculiar to him; it was part of the tradition of the Church as he knew it.

There are other signs also that Paul saw in the Servant of the fourth Servant Song a description of Christ. They are to be found in the tenth chapter of his Letter to the Romans, a closely argued and difficult passage. The purpose of the chapter is to show that Christ was preached to the Jews in the days of Isaiah, that this gospel was then ignored, and that God had warned the Jews that he would call the Gentiles into his covenant as well. In verse 8, Paul quotes Moses as saying in Deuteronomy 30.14:

But the word is near you; on your lips and in your heart,

and Paul adds:

that is, the word of faith, which we preach.

Strange as it may seem to us, Paul believed that faith in Christ was preached in Old Testament times. Then in verse 13 he quotes Joel 2.32:

[1] Compare also Hebrews 2.5-18, which seems to follow the same pattern.

every one who calls upon the name of the Lord will be saved.

His comment:

how are men to call upon him in whom they have not believed?

shows that he takes 'Lord' here as meaning Christ. And he goes on to say in effect that men in Old Testament times did have an opportunity of hearing about Christ, and therefore of believing in him. The proof of this comes in verse 15, where he calls in Isaiah as a witness when the prophet says in Isaiah 52.7:

How beautiful are the feet of those who preach good news!

This shows that good news about Christ was preached in Isaiah's day. What is more, it was disbelieved, for Paul continues his commentary in verse 16:

But they have not all heeded the gospel; for Isaiah says, Lord, who has believed what he has heard from us?'

Paul here is quoting Isaiah 53.1. And his next remark makes it quite clear that Isaiah had a message about Christ, for Paul writes (verse 17):

So faith comes from what is heard, and what is heard comes by the preaching of Christ.

The copy of the book of Isaiah which Paul probably had open before him as he wrote this involved exegesis of Scripture would not have possessed the divisions into chapters and verses to which we are accustomed. The text of chapter 52 and 53 would for him be a continuous whole, and it is impossible to believe that he stopped short at 53.1 and refused to read on. In fact, he indicates clearly enough that what follows Isaiah 53.1 is Isaiah's message, and that that message was what he calls 'the preaching of Christ'. Underlying this whole chapter, therefore, is the conviction that in Isaiah's chapters 52 and 53 we have a description of Jesus Christ.

Two other New Testament writers present us with the theme of Jesus as the Servant. The first is the author of I Peter. The picture of Jesus as the Suffering Servant in Second Isaiah meets us on almost every page of this epistle. Indeed, no book in the New Testament has more to say on this theme. The Servant of the Lord is, in fact, the image that the author of the epistle primarily uses in order to express the meaning of Jesus' death. If we could be certain that the author of the epistle is St Peter himself, this would of course be first-hand evidence for Jesus' conception of his own vocation. But we cannot be certain of this. Many scholars would place the epistle in the last quarter of the first century AD. As such, its evidence is most valuable as an interpretation, and it certainly indicates a tradition older than itself.[1]

Secondly, when we come to study the theme of the Servant in the fourth gospel, we find ourselves in much the same uncertainty as is created by the problem of the authorship of I Peter. I have deliberately refrained from siting this gospel as original evidence for Jesus' conception of his own vocation. This is not because its evidence is valueless, but because it is impossible at this point in the development of New Testament scholarship to be certain about the historical character of the fourth gospel. Does it contain original historical material on a par with the evidence of the first three gospels?[2] Or is it wholly an interpretation of the material found in these gospels? Because this question is so difficult and obscure, we must not cite the evidence of the fourth gospel as an original witness to historical facts about Christ. But John's interpretation of the

---
[1] The Petrine authorship is by no means indenfensible, as is the case for example with II Peter. Some scholars suggest that an original baptismal address of Peter has been incorporated in an epistle by a disciple of Peter.

[2] I personally believe it is based on original historical material but it would be much too complicated a task to give my reasons within the limits of this book.

significance of Christ is very valuable evidence in itself, in the way that Paul's evidence is valuable, that is as a help to our understanding of the full meaning of the life, death, and resurrection of Jesus Christ.

John certainly underlines the element of service in the career of Jesus. He does it in typical fashion by substituting for an account of the institution of the Lord's Supper an account of Jesus washing the disciples' feet. This is not because he was not interested in the Christian Eucharist (there is ample evidence in his gospel that he was), but because he wishes to sum up in this incident the deepest significance of Jesus' coming. He introduces the incident in 13.1 with a sentence which sums up Jesus' whole life:

> Now before the feast of the Passover, when Jesus knew that his hour had come to depart out of this world to the Father, having loved his own who were in the world, he loved them to the end.

Humble service is the keynote of Jesus' life, and it was to be the keynote of the disciples' life also.[1]

In the gospels and in the epistles, therefore, the Servant theme is central both in Jesus' interpretation of his own vocation, and in the first disciples' understanding of his meaning for the world. Within this theme, the description of the Suffering Servant of the last Servant Song has its place. It must be seen in the perspective of the whole succession of the servants of God, who 'have been since the world began', and whose work is brought to perfection in the life, death and resurrection of Jesus Christ.

[1] Evidence could be shown that John specifically understood the Servant Songs as a description of Christ. A comparison of Isaiah 49.3 and 52.13 in the Greek with John 3.14; 8.28; 12.32-34; 13.31-32; 14.13; 15.8 suggests very strongly that John drew the key concepts of 'lifting up' and 'glorifying' from these passages in Isaiah and that therefore he identified Christ with the Servant of the Lord.

3

OURSELVES AS YOUR SERVANTS

THERE IS a story told about a letter to a bishop from one of his clergy. It ran something like this:

My Lord, I understand that the diocesan authorities wish me to take over a certain parish in another part of the diocese. I must make it clear that I have no intention of doing this, and I may add that I will not consent, even if you order me to do so.
 I am, my Lord, your most obedient servant . . .

Yet the very word 'minister' represents the Greek *diakonos*, one of the words used to describe the Servant-Messiah in the New Testament. What is more, some passages in the New Testament explicitly describe the relation of the ordained ministry towards the Church in terms of humble service.

St Paul is the great authority for us here, and this is not surprising, as it is really only in his letters that we have any detailed account of the life of the local church in New Testament times. We get tiny glimpses in I Peter, in the Johannine Epistles, and in Hebrews, but they cannot be compared with the intimate picture of Paul at work in the churches he founded which we can find in his letters.

It may seem an anachronism to speak of 'the relation of the ordained ministry towards the Church' as I did above, when we are only thinking about Paul and his converts. Was there really an ordained ministry as early as that? We need not argue about whether, or how, Paul was ordained, but he certainly considered that he and his fellow-workers had a special pastoral relationship to their converts. In many ways the best analogy to this relationship is to be found today among the younger churches, founded within the last hundred years. Paul was primarily a missionary, which in itself establishes a link with the Servant of the Lord. As a missionary, he was not working on his own, but was supported by a group of assistants without whose help he could never have carried on his work. We know the names of many of them: Timothy, Titus, Apollos, Silas, Epaphroditus. But there were many more whose names we do not know, sometimes referred to as 'the brethren' (e.g. I Corinthians 16.11). This missionary group with Paul as its leader is the New Testament equivalent of the ordained ministry of today, and it is significant for us that Paul describes this group as carrying out in some sense the work of servants in the Church.

There are three main passages where this thought is to be found, all of them in the Corinthian epistles. Each is a long passage extending over more than a dozen verses, so that they cannot be printed in full. But it will help the reader to have his Bible open as he reads the following brief commentaries on each.

1. *I Corinthians 3.18-4.13*

Paul is dealing with a difficult situation in Corinth. The Church is split into parties, and each party takes the name of some leader. There is a Peter party, and an Apollos party, and a Paul party; there is also probably a party which sanctimoniously claims to be Christ's party (see 1.10-17). These party loyalties have not been encouraged by those after whom they have been named; obviously Paul holds no grudge against Apollos. Still less has he organized the Paul party himself! What he has to show the Corinthians is that these various missionaries, whom they are using as convenient excuses for mutual antagonisms, are in the Church ultimately in order to serve the Church. The Corinthians' attempt to put them into the position of faction leaders is based on the unspoken assumption that the missionaries really wish to 'domineer over those in their charge' (see I Peter 5.3). Indeed, it is almost as if the Corinthian Christians, who were probably mostly Gentiles, were giving a living illustration of what Christ said about them in Luke 22.25-26:

> The kings of the Gentiles exercise lordship over them; and those in authority over them are called benefactors. But not so with you; rather let the greatest among you become as the youngest, and the leader as one who serves.

Paul therefore begins by a warning against that sort of worldly wisdom which the Corinthians seemed to value highly (3.18), and leads on in 3.21-22 to a reminder of the startling fact that 'all things are yours'. He could hardly have put the true situation more effectively: these missionaries, whom the Corinthians thought would respond to the stimulus of worldly ambition, are in fact only there in order to serve the Corinthians. More than that, the Corinthians are lords over the whole world and the entire future—with one all-important reservation. They have all this in Christ. Though all things and all ministers belong to them, they belong to Christ.

Paul then goes on to show what this means in their actual lives:

> This is how one should regard us, as servants of Christ, and stewards of the mysteries of God.

We cannot fail to see here that Paul is in some sense putting himself and his helpers on one side, and the Corinthians on the other, not in order to prove the superiority of the ministry (quite the reverse); but in order to show what being a servant of Christ really means in practice. The word for 'servant' here is one we have not yet met. It does not imply a slave, but rather a subordinate. Similarly a steward is someone to whom a trust is given by a superior. Paul is careful to emphasize in 4.2-5 that he does not regard himself as appointed by the Corinthians and therefore he is not responsible to them. He is responsible only to God. We have here therefore a strange situation: the ministers (Paul and Apollos specifically, but all the other apostles and missionaries are in the background of his mind) are there for the purpose of serving the Church. They are also and at the same time servants of Christ. How is this double service to be adjusted? And what of the Corinthians? How are they to serve? Paul answers these questions in the passage that follows, 4.6-13.

In verses 6-7, he reminds them that their privileged position, referred to in 3.21-22, is not something they have earned, but is a free gift of God:

If then you have received it, why do you boast as if it were not a gift?

Then he proceeds to draw (8-13) a strange contrast between the Corinthians on the one hand and the apostles on the other. By the 'apostles' he must mean primarily himself and Apollos; that is clear from verse 16. The Corinthians, he says, are delighted with themselves; they feel they are enlightened Christians on top of the world. They can even afford to patronise men like Paul and Apollos as they carry out their strenuous ministry. The apostles, on the other hand, are right in the thick of the struggle: as they wage their destined conflict against the forces of darkness, they feel like condemned criminals dragged to public execution. They have no time to look after their own dignity, as the Corinthians have. They must accept the hardships that their chosen way of life holds in store for them, scant rations, inadequate clothing, many a penalty from public authorities, no fixed home—and on top of it all they must even make enough money in their spare time to support themselves. They meet abuse with blessing, persecution with patience, lies with conciliatory words. They are treated like the dregs of society, the scapegoats of everybody's sins.

And as Paul's picture of the life of the apostles grows and becomes clear to the mind, it is plain that it is in fact an imitation of the life of Christ himself. Feature after feature seem to belong primarily to Christ. The apostles 'are like men sentenced to death'; Christ *was* sentenced to death. They are 'a spectacle to the world': we think of Christ carrying his cross to Golgotha in the sight of all Jerusalem. They are 'fools for Christ's sake' and 'weak', compared to the 'strong' Corinthians. We think of I Corinthians 1.25, where Paul refers to the cross as 'the foolishness of God' and the 'weakness of God'. The apostles 'hunger and thirst, are buffeted and homeless'; so was Christ.

> When reviled, we bless; when persecuted, we endure; when slandered, we try to conciliate.

All this applies even more obviously to Christ; and the word for 'try to conciliate' (one word in Greek) is the same as is translated 'making his appeal' in II Corinthians 5.20, and there it is used to describe God's redeeming action in Christ. Finally, those two words 'refuse' and 'offscouring' have a definitely sacrificial significance in Greek religious vocabulary.

From this comparison two important conclusions follow: first, the life of the ministry reproduces in the Church the life of Christ. Christ lived a life of humble self-giving; these verses might well be called a description of the Servant-Messiah's life. The primary task of the ministry, it seems, is to carry out the ministry of the Servant in the Church. Secondly, the purpose of this task is that the Church as a whole should live out Christ's atoning life in the world. Paul is being heavily ironic in this passage; he does not really praise the Corinthians for their superior attitude. He is really trying to shame them into coming down from their comfortable seats at the ringside into the arena. They should be down there in the dust of conflict, at the side of the apostles. The apostles do not carry out this Servant ministry just in order that the rest of the Church may stand idly by; in 4.16, Paul says: 'I urge you, then, be imitators of me. . . .'

We have here a profound exposition of the relation of the ordained ministry to the Church. The ministers must carry out Christ's ministry of humble service, so that the Church may be drawn into the same ministry.

2. *II Corinthians 4.1-15*

The third chapter of Corinthians is one of the most obscure in all Paul's writings, but the main outline is clear. Paul is comparing the new dispensation inaugurated by the coming of the Messiah in the flesh, with the old, which had been inaugurated by the meditation of Moses. This leads him on to compare the new ministry (the word he uses is *diakonia*) with the old, and the new ministers (he calls them ministers, *diakonoi*, of the new covenant, see 3.6) with the minister of the old Moses. In the third chapter he seems to be looking at them rather from the outside, contrasting the ministry as a whole with Moses' ministry. Now in chapter 4 he turns to the internal operation of the ministry of the new covenant. What does it actually do in the Church?

In 4.5 Paul writes:

For what we preach is not ourselves, but Jesus Christ as Lord, with ourselves as your servants for Jesus' sake.

The word for 'servants' here is not *diakonoi* but *douloi,* which means slaves. And the ministers are slaves for Jesus' sake. This means not only that the ministers serve because Jesus wishes them to (though it does mean that), but that they are servants because Jesus was the Servant first. They serve the Church because Jesus serves the Church. Again, we can trace in verses 5-12 the same pattern of duty which we found laid down for the Servant in Second Isaiah, and for Jesus in the gospels: obedience, witness, suffering. Obedience is implied in the word 'servants'. Witnessing is necessarily involved in preaching Jesus Christ as Lord, witnessing to prophecy fulfilled and to the mighty acts of God in Christ. And suffering is immediately afterwards described in verses 8-12.

In 4.10-12 Paul works out in greater detail what the suffering life of the ministry involves in terms of Christ, the ministers and the Church. We cannot fail to see that in some real sense the life of Christ is to be reproduced in the life of the ministry:

always carrying about in the body the death of Jesus, so that the life of Jesus may also be manifested in our bodies.

This life of Jesus that the ministers reproduce is also the death of Jesus, the dying life that produces life in others. And so the interchange goes on. Jesus gave his life that we might have life; the ministers are to reproduce the life of Jesus by dying themselves in this life; and this will mean life for the Church whom they serve (verse 12). There is an interesting link in verse 11:

For while we live we are always being given up to death for Jesus sake.

That phrase 'we are being given up' (one word in the Greek) recalls what Paul wrote in I Corinthians 11.23:

For I received what I also delivered to you, that the Lord Jesus on the night when *he was betrayed*, took bread. . . .

'He was betrayed' is the same verb in Greek as is used to express 'we are being given up' here. The meaning is not an implied hit at Judas' treachery, but a reminder that the death of Jesus and the death-in-life of the ministers are equally part of God's plan. Finally, death-in-life and life-through-death is ultimately for the sake of the Church (verse 12):

> So death is at work in us, but life in you.

And now in verses 13-14 Paul takes us a stage deeper in his thought. Here is the translation of the RSV:

Since we have the same spirit of faith as he had who wrote 'I believed, and so I spoke', we too believe, and so we speak.

But this version obscures the true meaning of what Paul wrote, for the Greek is literally: 'Having the same spirit of faith, according as it is written . . . etc.' If we read it according to the RSV, we understand it to be David (or the author of the psalm) who believed and spoke. It seems more in accordance with Paul's thought that the speaker of these words should be Christ. This is confirmed when we look at the psalm which Paul quotes. He actually refers to Psalm 116.10, but we must also read what follows. Here is a translation of Psalm 116.10-19 as Paul would have had it in the Greek version of the Old Testament:

> I believed, therefore did I speak;
>   but I was greatly humbled.
> I said in my excitement
>   'Every man is a liar'.
> What shall I repay unto the Lord
>   in return for all he has rewarded me?
> I will take the cup of salvation
>   and I will call upon the name of the Lord.
> Valuable before the Lord
>   is the death of his holy ones.
> O Lord, I am thy servant,
>   they servant and the son of thy handmaid.
> Thou has broken my bonds asunder.
>   I will sacrifice to thee the sacrifice of thanksgiving.
> I will repay my vows to the Lord,
>   before all his people,
> In the courts of the house of the Lord,
>   in the midst of thee, Jerusalem.

I suggest that Paul sees this entire passage as the prophetic utterance of the Messiah, and that he is claiming to model his faith not on David, or on anyone whom we might have imagined to have written the psalm, but on Christ himself. We know that this kind of interpretation is very much in line with Paul's approach to the Old Testament. We are not concerned with the question: was this kind of interpretation justified? The point that matters for us is: what light does it throw on Paul's belief about Jesus? Paul sees Jesus in this psalm as showing faith, as being greatly humbled, as experiencing salvation from God, as referring to the value of his death, as calling himself the Servant of the Lord, as giving thanks to God for his resurrection:

> Thou hast broken my bonds asunder
> I will sacrifice to thee the sacrifice of thanksgiving.

and finally as praising God in the Church. Paul would take 'Jerusalem' in the psalm as a reference to the Church: see Galatians 4.26.

This interpretation is confirmed by three things. In Psalm 116.16, the writer calls himself a *doulos* of God, and Paul has just used this word of those who minister for Christ's sake. Secondly, in the same verse, the Psalmist makes a reference to his bonds being broken, which Paul would see as a prophecy of the resurrection. In II Corinthians 4.14 Paul writes:

knowing that he who raised the Lord Jesus will raise us also with Jesus.

This seems a natural inference: as Jesus had faith and spoke, so Paul (and his companions) had faith and spoke. And as Jesus' faith was answered by the resurrection, so will the faith of the ministers be answered by their being raised. Thirdly, the psalm ends with an act of praise in Jerusalem, and in verse 15 Paul goes on to speak of the thanksgivings of the Church.

By this reference to Psalm 116 Paul has bound the life of the ministry and the life of Christ even more closely together. Not only does the life of the ministry reproduce the life of Christ, but the life of Christ offers in itself the pattern of salvation. Christ is not only the Saviour, but also himself the first to be saved, and the one because the other. Verse 15 sets the crown on Paul's astonishing argument:

> For it is all for your sake, so that as grace extends to more and more people it may increase thanksgiving, to the glory of God.

The whole process, Christ's life and death, the ministers' death-in-life, is all for the sake of the Church: not that the Church is to stand by applauding, but that it may take part, it also may enter on this dying life, may experience that salvation which is life through death, may in turn acknowledge itself to be God's servant, and may come to the act of thanksgiving which is really Christ praising the Father in the Church.

It is no coincidence at all that Paul's word for 'thanksgiving' is *eucharistia*, the word which the Church from the second century onward used for the Lord's Supper. Viewed from one angle, the Eucharist is simply Christ giving thanks to God in his brethren. Thus we find the thought of the Servant central in the life of Christ, in the life of the ministry, in the life of the Church, and in the Church's sacramental worship.

3. *II Corinthians 5.14-6.10*

Between II Corinthians 4.16 and this third passage, Paul has been looking ahead and describing the nature of the resurrection body. Now he returns to the theme of the ministry of the new covenant, and treats especially the subject of the reconciliation.

In 5.14-15 we see again the interchange between Christ and Christians:

We are convinced that one has died for all; therefore all have died. And he died for all, that those who live might live no longer for themselves, but for him who for their sake died and was raised.

This phrase 'one has died for all; therefore all died' recalls the prophecies of Second Isaiah, where the Servant was both the people and the individual, and even when plainly only the individual could be meant, the individual was presented as acting on behalf of the people. In verse 16 that phrase 'from a human point of view' has given much trouble to commentators. The same phrase in Romans 4.1 is translated 'according to the flesh'. The meaning here seems to be that Paul is not content to see Jesus Christ just as a character in history. He sees him with the eyes of faith as the Messiah, as the Son of God, above all as the Servant, disguised by the very fact of the humble status which he has assumed. This leads on well to the theme of the reconciliation which Jesus has achieved, for, as verse 21 shows, the deed could only be attempted by One who was willing to identify himself so closely with sinful men that he was not fully recognized for what he was till after his death.

Verses 18-19 now explicitly mention the 'ministry of reconciliation'. Twice in these verses Paul says that this ministry was given by God to us. To what group do the words 'we' and 'us' refer? It cannot be to Paul alone as an individual, as if Paul were using the royal 'we'. The Queen, for example, may say 'we are graciously pleased', but she could not say 'we are ambassadors' in the plural, as Paul does in verse 20. Does it refer then to the ministers, the apostles? Yes, it certainly does, but the real question is: is it limited to them? In verse 20 this would seem to be the truth, for the ambassadors beseech the Corinthians to be reconciled to God. But it would entirely frustrate the purpose of this great act of divine reconciliation if the ministry of reconciliation were to be confined to the ordained ministers. We would be back again at the situation which Paul ironically describes in I Corinthians 4, where the main body of the Church are passive spectators of the forward march of the gospel So we have here what we have met in the two other passages: the activity of God in Christ is taken up by the ministers, and by them passed on to the Church.

Now we approach the very centre of Paul's argument, obscure because of the very paradox of the divine action. Verse 20 runs:

So we are ambassadors for Christ, God making his appeal through us. We beseech you on behalf of Christ, be reconciled to God.

We have already noticed the connection of this passage with I Corinthians 4.12. There the apostles, when slandered 'try to conciliate'. Here not only the apostles, but God himself tries to conciliate—but the RSV here translates the word 'conciliate' as 'making his appeal'. Here is the suggestion that Christ, in coming as Servant, was actually representing the character of God himself. He did not assume the character of Servant simply as a means to an end. In some sense God himself is a Servant-God, at least a God who, far from threatening or even commanding, humbly entreats. This does not mean that he is powerless, or that the Servant has no authority. The Servant has all power and authority committed to him, and hence, as we shall see, the Servant-Church wields authority also. But behind that is the God who humbly entreats through his servant-ministers.

Finally Paul moves to the greatest and most outrageous paradox of all in verse 21:

For our sake he made him to be sin who knew no sin, so that in him we might become the righteousness of God.

This is perhaps the most difficult single text in the New Testament: the most appalling precipices yawn on either side for all who attempt an interpretation. There is a danger that we may either find ourselves accusing Jesus of being a sinner, or else suggest that for his own purpose God regarded him as a sinner.

It seems that Paul is here outlining the very ultimate degree of Christ's self-identification with us, the very lowest point to which he condescended when he took the form of a slave. He allowed himself (God allowed him) to be accounted sin by the Law. He refused to do what orthodox Jews of his day thought God had commanded them to do, seek to gain credit with God by keeping the Law. He lived by faith not Law (see 4.13) and therefore repudiated the Law and the path of self-justification. He said to the Jews once (Mark 10.18):

> Why do you call me good? No one is good but God alone.

Here is another way of expressing what Paul says in the hymn of the incarnation in Philippians 2.7:

> He emptied himself, taking the form of a servant.

We said on page 39 that in the Greek 'he emptied himself' is a literal translation of the phrase in Isaiah 53.12 which the RSV renders 'he poured out his soul to death'. An equally possible translation of the Hebrew would be 'he stripped himself'. Here Paul shows the amazing extent of the stripping. He stripped himself even of that claim to moral goodness which would have distinguished him from sinners. Short of becoming a sinner (and Paul shows that this idea is repudiated), how could God come closer to us sinners? Here the Servant is shown us at his very humblest.

We are reminded of something else Christ said. In Luke 17 7-10 we have that vivid parable of the farmer coming in from a day's work in the fields and telling his servant to prepare supper. Jesus' comment is this:

> So you also, when you have done all that is commanded you, say, 'We are unworthy servants; we have only done what was our duty'.

Christ renounced his own merit in order that we might realize our own real lack of it.

In chapter 6, verses 3-10, Paul elaborates the theme of the servant ministry in a way to which he has accustomed us. His words in 6.4:

> as servants of God we commend ourselves in every way,

show us that this servant theme is never far from Paul's thought. The word he used here is *diakonoi,* no doubt because he has used *diakonia* for 'ministry' in the previous verse. Verses 4 and 5 emphasise the sufferings and hardship of the ministry; verses 8-10 return to the great theme of the dying ministry. In a series of brilliant paradoxes, Paul drives home the equation of the ministers' life with that of Christ. Practically every phrase in these two verses could be as well applied to Christ. The last phrase in verse 10 is:

> as having nothing, and yet possessing everything.

This gives us in a word Christ himself as he hung on the cross. He had given up everything, stooped down to the status of a condemned and executed criminal, deliberately accepted the condemnation of the law, and because of it (not despite it) had gained the victory which made him Lord of all.

In this third passage, the place of the Church as a whole may not be easy to discern, but it is there. The Church is the end of the process. There is no suggestion that the ministers are set to carry out the life of Christ in a way which is impossible for the Church. In the whole three passages we have been studying there is nothing said of the ministry that could not be said of the Church as a whole, or even of any individual Christian. Thus it is clear that, if the ministers are to be servants of the Servant, then the Church as a whole must be a servant also. This is not to suggest that the ministry is unnecessary, or a mere preliminary arrangement which the mature Church can discard. This is not at all the impression Paul gives. As we shall be seeing in the next chapter, the ministry has real authority, and so had the Church as a whole. But the ministry is not independent of the Church; it is there in order to enable the Church to be the Church of the Servant.

This is well brought out in the last passage we will look at here, Ephesians 4.11-14. As in Philippians 2 and Romans 15, Paul is here calling the brethren to united action and thought. He emphasizes in 4.1-6 the unity of the Church, the great fundamentals that bind all Christians together. Then in verses 7-11 he speaks of the various gifts that the ascended Christ has given to his Church, and it is plain that of these gifts the ordained ministry is one. Verses 11-12 run:

And his gifts were that some should be apostles, some prophets, some evangelists, some pastors and teachers, for the equipment of the saints, for the work of ministry (*diakonia*), for building up the body of Christ.

As in 4.13 (p. 52), so here we must take exception to the RSV rendering. The RSV puts a comma between 'saints' and 'for the work of ministry'. This implies that the various ministers are given to the Church for three purposes: (a) for equipping the saints, (b) for the work of ministry, (c) for building up the body. In fact in the Greek the probability is that (a) and (b) are not two parallel objects, but one. The New English Bible rendering takes it this way:

to equip God's people for work in his service.

This expresses it neatly and agrees with what Paul has been teaching in the two Corinthian Epistles. The ordained ministry is given by God to the Church in order to equip the Church as a whole for its work.

Here, then, is the climax of the Scriptural argument. *The Servant Messiah carries out his ministry in the lives of his ministers. His life is reproduced in their lives, so they also are servants. But this ministry is exercised in and towards the Church, so as to enable the Church itself to carry out the ministry of the Servant. The Messiah came as a Servant; his ministers are servants; and the Church he created is a Servant-Church.*

4

THE AUTHORITY OF THE SERVANT

ARE MINISTERS just laymen who have lost their amateur status? So wrote the late T. W. Manson in a posthumously published book. The question brilliantly pinpoints a problem which must now be faced. We have spoken much about the servant status of both ministry and Church. What about their *authority*? Does either ministry or Church have a legitimate authority according to the New Testament? Today in the West all authority is at a discount, but most of all church authority. In the Free Churches the original Reformers' acceptance of the authority of the ministry is rarely heard of. In Anglicanism, if a bishop begins to exercise authority over either clergy or laity, there are those who will at once denounce him. Even in the more tightly disciplined Church of Rome, laymen are daring publicly to contradict the utterance of the hierarchy more frequently than in the past. Yet the New Testament witnesses unmistakeably to the fact that both ministry and Church possess Christ's authority.

St Paul on Authority

There are points to notice in St Paul's letters, which were, after all, written down at least twenty years earlier than either the first gospel or the fourth. Throughout I Corinthians Paul constantly speaks with authority as if he expected to be heard and obeyed. In 4.15 he seems to claim a father's authority:

For I became your father in Christ Jesus through the gospel.

And on the basis of this, he can say in verse 21:

> What do you wish? Shall I come to you with a rod?

If we read the whole of chapter five of this letter, we cannot fail to recognize that he is both exercising discipline and claiming authority in the Church which he founded. Similarly in chapter seven, he is frequently giving them instructions on difficult matters connected with marriage. It is true that he distinguishes in 7.10 between what he has to say and what the Lord said, obviously giving superior authority to the latter. In 7.25 and 40 he bases his advice on his own experience and commission, but still it comes as very authoritative advice. In chapter eleven he is even more explicit: he commends the Corinthians on certain points (11.2), but later speaks about 'instructions' (v. 17) and does not hesitate to condemn:

> But in the following instructions I do not commend you . . .

Paul at least believed that as an apostle he had authority over the church which he had helped to found.

In II Corinthians Paul emphasizes the note of authority even more strongly, because his authority has been challenged and openly flouted. In chapters 10-13 of that letter he is writing with great passion, and even menace. Here is what he says in 10.5-6 (NEB), for example:

> We demolish sophistries and all that rears its proud head against the knowledge of God; we compel every human thought to surrender in obedience to Christ; and we are prepared to punish all rebellion when once you have put yourselves in our hands.

The final words of this part of the letter (12.19-13.10) are the sternest that Paul ever wrote as far as we know. The threat of excommunication is in the background all the time. It is very interesting also to learn from 2.1-9 that the local Church could exercise discipline over one member. Paul is actually at this point deprecating further discipline:

For such a one this punishment by the majority is enough.[1]

We find similar language being used about the local ministry. It seems clear that in the Churches founded by Paul there were certain individuals who had pastoral authority. We do not know for certain by what name they were known. Philippians 1.1 suggests that they may have been called *episkopoi*, though in I Peter 5.1 they are called *presbyteroi*. Whatever their title, they seem to have existed as the local ministry, exercising supervision over the local Church. Of course any notion of a paid, full-time ministry would be absurd. In I Thessalonians 5.12-13 Paul says this about them:

> But we beseech you, brethren, to respect those who labour among you and are over you in the Lord and admonish you, and to esteem them very highly in love because of their work.

The word for 'labour' here is frequently used of pastoral work amongst Christians. A very similar exhortation occurs in I Corinthians 16.15-16. Paul refers to the household of Stephanas and says that they have

> devoted themselves to the service (*diakonia*) of the saints.

Paul urges the Corinthians 'to be subject to such men'. Here is *diakonia*, but it involves authority. We find the same thing probably at a slightly later period in Hebrews 13.17:

> Obey your leaders and submit to them.

And I Peter 5.1-5 gives us a little charge to the elders in the churches to which the Letter is written, where we find the phrase already quoted on p. 47:

> not as domineering over those in your charge, but being examples to the flock.

Plainly, the local ministry also had authority. This also emerges

[1] There is good reason to believe that chapters 1-9 of this epistle actually represent a separate letter written after chapters 10-13.

in Paul's address to the local ministry in Ephesus (Acts 20.17-38).

The group of founding missionaries exercised authority over the Churches which they founded; and the local ministry had authority in the local Church. What about the Church as a whole? Does it exercise authority? This is much more difficult to decide, as there are very few instances in the New Testament where the authority of the whole Church comes into question.

The most obvious example is the council at Jerusalem described in Acts 15. This should give us clear guidance, but in fact it does not. The whole incident is surrounded by historical problems. The council seems to consist of 'the apostles and elders' (Acts 15.6). But the summing up seems to have been delivered by James the brother of the Lord. Was he an apostle? We do not know. The final decision is made by 'the apostles and elders with the whole Church' (15.22), which certainly looks like an authoritative decision of the Church. But what happened to the decision? If the epistle to the Galatians was written subsequently, then the decision seems to have carried no authority for either Paul or the Galatian Christians, for he makes no reference to a decision which would have counted heavily in his favour. Even if Galatians was written (as many scholars believe) just before the council met, we still find no trace of the council's authority in I Corinthians and Romans. Yet both these letters deal with the very questions on which the council pronounced, and both must have been written after the council took place.

Perhaps all that can be said is that some council, perhaps of local authority only, took place. It shows at least that when Luke wrote Acts, it was considered quite natural for the Church as a whole to exercise its authority by means of a council.

Authority in the Gospels

Equally difficult is the famous passage Matthew 16.17-19. This is an addition by the author of the first gospel to Mark's narrative of the incident at Caesarea Philippi. In Mark 8.27-9.1, Jesus asks his disciples whom do men think he is. This brings out Peter's great confession, 'you are the Christ'. Immediately after this Jesus warns his disciples of his coming sufferings and death, and of the need for his followers to deny themselves and accept his death also. Matthew's gospel has all this, but after Peter's confession comes a special charge to Peter. The truth of Jesus' Messiahship has been revealed to Peter by God himself. On Peter, Christ will build his Church; Peter is to receive the keys of the kingdom, and whatever he binds on earth will be bound in heaven.

This passage has occasioned more controversy than any other in the Bible. Roman Catholics see in it one of the main proofs of their doctrine of the supreme authority of the Pope, Peter's successor as Bishop of Rome. Protestants have tended in the past to say that the promise is given to Peter's faith, not to Peter personally; and in more recent years to deny altogether that Jesus could have uttered these words. These are extreme views, and others are also possible. We can hardly claim to have the exact words of Jesus here, for we are not accustomed to find him elsewhere thinking in terms of 'I will build my Church'. But behind these words there must be actual teaching of Jesus. Probably Peter is here taken as a representative of believing humanity: he has seen the Messiah in the Servant and this faith is the distinguishing mark of Jesus' disciples. Authority (this is the meaning of 'binding and loosening') is shown here as given to the group of Jesus' disciples and hence to the Church. There is no intention to connect that authority with one see or one place. In short, the most we can say with

c

confidence about this passage is that here Jesus gives authority to the Church—but that much we can affirm.

The other great passage is John 20.19-23. The risen Christ meets the disciples, and says to them:

> As the Father has sent me, even so send I you.

Then he breathes on them and adds:

Receive the Holy Spirit. If you forgive the sins of any, they are forgiven; if you retain the sins of any, they are retained.

This is certainly another case of St John giving us an alternative account of a gospel incident, and is probably also his version of Pentecost. It is certainly his version of Matthew 28.16-20. There are some interesting points to note. Throughout his gospel John never refers to the Twelve as apostles, and does not actually describe the disciples in the Upper Room, either before or after the Resurrection, as 'the Twelve'. It therefore seems likely that he is anxious to make clear the relation of Christ to the Church as a whole rather than to the ministry alone. This is certainly true of John 17, where Jesus prays for the Church, present in the disciples who were with him in the Upper Room, and yet to come, in his divine foreknowledge. Consequently it seems very likely that John here means to represent Christ as formally giving his authority to the Church as a whole. We cannot doubt that this is what actually happened, though we cannot say whether the first gospel, the fourth gospel or Acts gives the most accurate account of the event.

Here, then, is an important fact that we must take into account as we turn to the second part of this study, the application to the Church's life of the witness of Scripture. We have up to this point been laying stress on the Servant rôle which Christ came to play, and the consequent humble vocation of both ministry and Church. But after all, Jesus when he was on earth had great authority. Mark says (Mark 1.22):

he taught them as one who had authority, and not as the scribes.

It is only to be expected that the paradox of the Servant Messiah, who came to serve but claimed authority over men's whole personalities, should be reflected in the paradox of the ministers who are slaves for Christ's sake and yet claim obedience from those they serve; and the paradox of the Church which is set to carry out the service its Lord came to do, and yet possesses authority to bind and loose on earth.

This great paradox sets up the problem that we must try to work out in the ensuing chapters. Nowhere has it been better put than in John 13.12-16:

Now when he had washed their feet and taken his garments, and resumed his place, he said to them: 'Do you know what I have done to you? You call me Teacher and Lord; and you are right, for so I am. If I then, your Lord and Teacher, have washed your feet, you also ought to wash one another's feet. Truly, truly, I say to you a servant (*doulos*) is not greater than his master; nor is he who is sent (*apostolos*) greater than he who sent him.'

II

THE CHURCH'S LIFE

5

THE SERVANT CHURCH

THERE USED to be in the house of the Archbishop of Dublin a table bearing on its surface a brass plate, on which the following words were inscribed:

At this table in 1869 W. E. Gladstone plotted the downfall of the Irish Church.

The table had apparently belonged to Gladstone during the period when he was planning the bill that brought about the disestablishment of the Church of Ireland. What is significant about the inscription from our point of view is that the partial disendowment of the Church is equated with its downfall. That is to say, the Church is thought of as existing mainly by virtue of its status and endowments. To remove them is to destroy the Church. Perhaps it is hardly fair to single out this anonymous defender of the Church of Ireland for invidious mention, because the attitude is so common, among laity quite as much as clergy. The Church, it is assumed, exists for its own sake: to maintain the fabric of the Church is the devout Christian's main aim and an attack on the Church's material possessions is an attack on the very life of the Church. It is a sign of the extent to which the Church has become self-centred.

Here is another example, taken from my experience abroad. Once some years ago I was talking to an Indian Christian in what was then Hyderabad State, in South India. At the time of our conversation there was very great political instability in the State. The Nizam of Hyderabad was attempting to maintain a régime entirely independent of the newly constituted

Dominion of India (it later became the Republic of India), and it seemed that at any moment hostilities might break out which could only have the effect of bringing the Nizam's régime to an end. I remarked to my Indian friend that I hoped the Dominion forces would soon take over the State, as we would then be rid of a very unsatisfactory régime. My friend was shocked. 'What!', he said, 'do you want the Nizam to go, who has proved such a good friend to the Christians?' It is true that the Nizam had been quite encouraging to the attempts of the Christian Church to evangelize Hindus (he was himself a Muslim), but what impressed me was the self-centredness of the attitude implied by my friend's remark. According to his view, it was better that fifteen million Hyderabadis should continue to be governed by an inefficient and reactionary régime, rather than that they should be rid of it at the cost of some uncertainty as to the material future of the Church. Here was the Church's rôle as servant entirely forgotten. The material convenience of the Church (which may have numbered 3 per cent of the population of Hyderabad) was more important than the material well-being of the State as a whole.

Obviously, when sentiments such as we have just described come naturally to the minds of devout Christians, the fact that the Church exists to carry out the ministry of the Servant has been entirely forgotten. But in fact, if what we have been discovering in the first part of this book is true, then Christians must become accustomed to looking at the Church in a completely different way. In any new situation, we must ask first not 'How will this affect the Church's material well-being?' but 'How will this affect the Church's ministry to the world?' And by 'the Church' we must mean the whole body—not just the clergy or those laity who happen to be directly employed by the Church. Is this the way in which most people, whether believers or not, think of the Church in the West? And does the Church in fact attempt to carry out such a ministry? Should we recognize it if it did?

Social Service by the Church

In the past the Church did visibly carry out a ministry to the world. Indeed in this respect it has a fine record. From the first, Christians were distinguished from non-Christians in time of trouble. For example, about the middle of the third century AD, Cyprian, bishop of Carthage in North Africa, wrote a small book on the subject of patience for the members of his flock. The occasion was an attack of plague in the city of Carthage. The plague was so severe that any who could do so left the city. That meant, in effect, that the rich ran away, while the poor remained at work because the alternative was to starve. In these circumstances Cyprian directed his flock not to leave the city, even if it was in their power to do so, but to stay and tend the sick, bury the dead, and encourage those who were as yet untouched by the plague. His flock obeyed him finely, and many non-Christians were deeply impressed by the self-sacrifice of the members of the Church. It was all the more remarkable because the plague came just after a sharp period of persecution by the government authorities in the course of which many Christians had been imprisoned and some had died as martyrs for the faith. Moreover, within a year or two the persecution was renewed and Cyprian himself martyred. But the service of the Church to the world was not withheld on account of this.

Similarly Christians may claim the credit of having invented the hospital. The idea seems to have started with Basil, bishop of Caesarea in Cappadocia in Asia Minor (modern Turkey). He organized so many different institutions for destitute, needy and sick people near his own dwelling-place, that the locality became quite a town on its own. Subsequently of course throughout Europe the Church became the only guardian and provider of education. Through the Dark Ages that descended on the West, roughly between 500 and 1000 AD, the Church maintained any learning and education that survived. The consequence was that, when the darkness thinned from about 1000 onwards, the Church found itself in complete charge of all education everywhere. So complete was the identification of learning with theological learning that the whole concept of teaching as a service done by the Church faded out. Education became something that the Church controlled and monopolised. So also with the service of healing and care for the poor. The Church has come to terms with society so completely that it was difficult to distinguish the Church from the world and it needed the lives and examples of men like Francis of Assisi to remind the Church that it was there to serve the world, not just to absorb the world. By the time of the reformation in the sixteenth century many devout Christians had come to think of the official Church as they nowadays think of secular society in the West—as something to be guarded against as a corrupting influence, something needing reform and redemption.

The Reformation was largely a lay movement, and in those countries where it was successful it brought about a gradual laicising of the various services which the Church had hitherto carried out. This was not necessarily a secularising process, but with the Enlightenment of the seventeenth and eighteenth centuries and the French Revolution, a movement began which deliberately took out of the hands of the Church much that had still remained a Church monopoly. In those countries in the West where the Reformation failed or never took place, it was not until the French Revolution and the ensuing conquest of Europe by Napoleon's armies that the process of secularisation began. When it did begin it went ahead more

THE SERVANT CHURCH 75

violently and rapidly than in other countries where the control of the Church had already been loosened for some time. The result of all these movements is that today in Western Europe the major forms of social service which for centuries had been carried on by the Church—hospitals, education, care for the needy and destitute—have been very largely taken out of the hands of the Church and are carried on by the State. The Welfare State as it is known in Britain is the clearest example of this. The State appears to be doing more efficiently and on a vaster scale what the Church had been trying to do for centuries. Only in a few old-fashioned corners, like the Republic of Eire, does the Church remain as a main channel of social services.

On the other hand, all the functions of service that have been taken from the Church in the West by the State are still being performed by the Church in many countries in Asia and Africa where both the Christian Church and the Welfare State are relatively new phenomena. Indeed, it might be said that the history of the Church's rôle in social service through the centuries in the West is being re-enacted at a much more rapid rate in many areas in Asia and Africa. Over by far the larger part of Africa south of the Sahara is was the Church that first provided any education or medical service at all. And still in some countries, such as Nigeria for instance, the Church (in the sense of all Christian denominations) provides the greater part of the country's education. So also in India, it was the various Christian missions that first opened hospitals and dispensaries, that pioneered in the care of lepers and of orphans and the destitute; and above all it was the Christian missions that first opened schools. The State of Kerala, for example, leads all the other states of India in literacy, having (I believe) a clear 10 per cent lead over any other state. This is because missionary work there began early, and made contact at once with a large body of indigenous Christians who readily assimilated the Western type of education provided by mission schools.

Up till recently these various agencies of social service, hospitals, schools, etc., have been regarded by all as institutions provided by the various Western missionary organisations that originally instituted them. They have thus retained in the eyes of those who attended them a distinctly foreign character. There has been wide appreciation of the self-sacrifice and love that lies behind them, and they have been understood for the most part as examples of Christian service undertaken by foreigners for the benefit of the nationals of the various countries where they have been established. And this is no doubt a genuine activity of the Servant Church. But only very recently have Christians both in the West and the East come to see that this not enough. This social service should appear as the activity of the Servant-Church in the country concerned.

Too often the impression conveyed has been that Christians in England are anxious to serve the people of India in the name of Christ. But surely it is Christians of Indian birth who should be doing this to the utmost of their resources? Consequently recent decades have seen strenuous efforts to make the various institutions of social service in the Church overseas really institutions which belong to, and are operated by, the Church. The difficulties involved in this process we shall be looking at in a later chapter; but here is one instance. I know of a hospital which has existed for at least fifty years in a large city in India. When I first visited it it was called 'The Church of England Zenana Missionary Society Hospital' (one can just imagine how much information this must have conveyed to the average Hindu!). Today it is called 'The Church of South India Hospital' and the change is not in name only. The senior doctor in charge is an Indian lady, and the committee that runs it is integrated in the diocesan organization.

But national Christians themselves are also undertaking their own forms of social service, very often fashioning new methods for themselves in the process. Somewhere on the border of Madras State and the Andhra State in South India is a small village called Deenabandhupuram. This is the scene of an experiment in Christian living on the part of an Indian presbyter of the Church of South India. He has purchased a fairly large plot of land, and runs a model farm on it, where he trains young Christian farmers in modern methods of agriculture. It is also a centre of evangelism and exhibits a deliberate pattern of Christian community life. Thus in a sense the Church in the West, though it is no longer able officially to undertake the huge amount of social service for which it was once responsible, has passed the torch on to the more recently founded Churches in the East. It is therefore much more easy in many parts of Asia and Africa to envisage the Church as the Servant-Church. It is still, as an organized body, carrying out much service for the community.

In the Welfare State

In the meantime, however, in the West the Church seems to be faced with the question: how is it to carry out Christ's ministry of healing the whole man in a community where most of its former activities of social service have been taken over by the State? We can lay aside at once one solution of the problem which may be something of a temptation: 'The State now looks after the body; the Church can concentrate on looking after the soul'. Such a division is totally alien to the religion of the New Testament. A Church which is only interested in men's souls and does not care for their bodies has forgotten the meaning of the Gospel, and is untrue to the example of its

Master. So the question still remains. Is it true that the Church has gradually been edged out of the activities of the community, so that it occupies only a marginal position now?

In the deepest sense the answer to this question is, No. The Church is there all the time right in the arena. But because the ways by which the Church carries out its calling of Servant in the Welfare State are so different from what took place in the past, it seems best to distinguish three ways by which the Church in the West is now carrying out its ministry to the world. First, it can still supplement the social services undertaken by State. For example, the Church of England still runs many schools aided by the State. Some denominations make very great efforts to retain the control of as many schools as possible. The Roman Catholic Church, for instance, follows a policy of retaining and building as many schools as it possibly can. How far this is the best method in the circumstances of deploying the resources for service which the Church possesses, is something which only an expert could decide. Again in many places the Church runs community centres, especially in new housing areas where a lot of people are congregated without local associations or deep roots. This is certainly something that the Church ought to be able to do better than the State. There are still forms of social service that are much more effectively carried out by the Church as such than by the State: the care of the lonely and the aged, for example. And the Church is still very active in caring for orphans, for delinquent children, for the disabled and handicapped. In all these areas the State, with its greater financial resources, has certainly the major share; but the Church does not at all look like being eliminated here. So there is still plenty of room for supplementary social service, not in distributing direct financial assistance so much as acting in those places where personal care, patience and understanding is needed.

Secondly, in the modern Welfare State the Church is beginning to find new methods of service. It needs to be said here that one of the reasons why the Church has in the past been deprived of its opportunities of direct social service, such as education, by an increasingly secular state has been that the Church did not make the best use of its opportunities or refused to extend them beyond the modest compass to which it was accustomed.[1] But the consequence of this has been that the administration of the social services in England has lacked any clear Christian basis. This did not appear so much at first, where the problem was mainly to abolish acute poverty and illiteracy. But with the full flowering of the Welfare State the relative absence of Christian insights has produced new problems. In these new problems there is an opportunity for new Christian service.

To take one simple example: there is the Samaritans' service. Modern industrial society seems to isolate people mentally and spiritually by bringing them together physically in vast urban masses. This service is for the help of those who are in danger of suicide or crime because of their loneliness. It puts at their disposal immediate help day and night, which can be summoned by telephone. It does, in fact, rescue many lonely people from desperation.

Another example is the work of Marriage Guidance Councils, which are now to be met with in every large town. The secularisation of society, and breakdown of such Christian community as used to exist in the West, have meant that many people have no standards and no convictions about marriage.

[1] One hundred and twenty years ago the Church of England had to be forcibly dispossesed of its monopoly of university education in England. Up till about that time the administration of nearly all the colleges in Oxford and Cambridge had been a monopoly of the clergy of the Established Church; and it cannot be said that for the previous century (at least) they had used their monopoly for the benefit of the community as a whole.

Very often what they need is not easy divorce but sensible advice and friendship. This is what the Marriage Guidance Councils exist to provide. They are not run by the churches, but have the active support and help of many convinced Christians.

There are many other new ways in which Christ's service can be carried out in our new unprecedented social system. Sometimes a single congregation will find some specific task of service to perform in its own locality. Indeed, local Christian Churches ought to be vigilant in finding such occasions of service. And all the time the great expression of Christ's care for the destitute, refugees and needy all over the world is going on, supported by the money, prayer and service of Christians in the West. Christian Aid (from Britain and elsewhere) and Church World Service (from the USA) are among the true glories of the Church today.

A well-known actress has described why she became an active member of the Church of England. She had a friend in the country who had been involved in serious trouble, but had no friends in her own neighbourhood. The actress said that she could only visit her friend occasionally, and wondered how she could find friends for her nearby. In desperation she wrote to the local Church of England vicar and asked whether he could find friends for the woman in trouble. The vicar called on the actresses's friend the moment he received the letter. He personally befriended her and saw to it that she was looked after by members of his flock, though she had never attended church. What so much impressed the actress was that this kindness was exercised towards those who had done nothing to evoke it. Here is an example of the Church's pastoral care at its best, and here is what is perhaps the central service of the Church which has gone on ever since Jesus came, and which, when truly exercised as in this instance, reflects the sort of service Jesus came to give as perhaps nothing else can.

Perhaps the need to provide this sort of service for large numbers of largely nominal Christians provides the last justification for the existence of an established Church in England. We all know the old epigram about the Englishman liking to have a church from which he can stay away; but while there is any sense at all in which England can be called a Christian country, it is perhaps right that one Church should feel an obligation to look after every member of the nation, whether they acknowledge the claims of that Church or not, and whether they accept any Christian belief or not.

It is difficult, it must be admitted, to define in terms of the New Testament Church the sort of service that a Church in a Western country provides today for the great majority of the nation who are not believers. It could, I suppose, come under the category of 'building up the body of Christ', the sort of service that the Church must provide for its own members. But how far are these nominal Christians members of Christ, and how far does the visit from the vicar, or the sick call in hospital, or even the provision of a Sunday School for the children of unbelievers, really bring them nearer to belief in Christ and active membership of the Church? On the other hand, to refuse any pastoral care to non-churchgoers cannot be right, as long as they expect it, or need it, or feel that they have a right to it. And it hardly needs emphasizing that pastoral care of the faithful, the people who do respond and come to Church, is a service that can never cease as long as the Church exists.

In any case this pastoral care of the non-churchgoers is not anything like effective all over the country. There are still large numbers of people, especially in industrial areas, who are virtually out of touch with any church. But it is surely significant that some of these unchurched multitudes seem to be finding a substitute for pastoral care in other quarters. Two very respectable figures in the social system have to some extent taken the place of the parson as the man to whom people resort in trouble. These are the family doctor and the family solicitor. Perhaps also the bank manager plays his part. None of these can be accused of having deliberately usurped the clergyman's place, but circumstances often put them in a position where it is they who have to give advice on what are really spiritual issues.

Besides these venerable figures, a number of other more modern characters are exercising something like a pastoral relationship towards people in trouble. There is the psychologist, that spiritual adviser of a scientific age. And even more recently the sociologist has sometimes come forward as the man with the really scientific answer to problems of personal relationships. Naturally the Church in the person of its ordained ministers tends to look with suspicion and jealousy on these new practitioners; and it is true that one cannot always be sure what ideal of service lies behind the activities of any given psychologist or sociologist. But clergy and ministers who object to these new disciplines, and attempt to discourage their activities, are fighting a losing battle. A far more fruitful attitude is to attempt co-operation, and above all to remember that the Church is not identical with the clergy. The right way to ensure that psychology and sociology are tools in the service of the Servant is to encourage convinced Christians to train as psychologists and sociologists.

What Hinders Service?

Before we end the account of what could be called the Church's corporate service, we should ask: what are the things which hinder that service most? I do not mean: what are the external obstacles placed in the way of the Church's service by an hostile world? But what is it *in the life of the Church itself* that prevents the world from recognizing it as the Servant Church?

A lot of nonsense has been talked about the Church's *wealth*. Some people would apparently like the Church to possess no property at all, and live from one day to the next in simple faith that the necessary money would be provided. I have met missionaries in India who lived like this and their service was not more powerful, but weaker, because of it. Nor should there be any objection to the Church using its money sensibly. Money is not wrong in itself, any more than power is wrong in itself. But undoubtedly a great disparity between the financial resources of one group of people and that of another makes it extraordinarily difficult for the rich to serve the poor. This may seem strange, but, after all, our Lord did once astonish his disciples by stressing the difficulty that the rich encounter in entering the kingdom of God.

This was borne in on me very vividly a few years ago when I met a delegation from a certain denomination in America who were visiting that part of the Indian Church where I was working. They were official delegates and I have reason to believe that they did very adequately represent the outlook and situation of the Church that sent them. They were full of goodwill and were most anxious to assess the actual circumstances, life, and needs of the Indian Church. But the standard of living to which they were accustomed in America was so vastly different from that of even the middle-class member of the Indian Church, that they were simply incapable of estimating the real circumstances and needs of those they met. Everything seemed to them so appallingly impoverished; what we knew to be comfortable middleclass houses seemed to them miserable hovels. What we considered the most comfortable method of travel money could buy seemed to them intolerably uncomfortable. With the best will in the world, their wealth had rendered them largely incapable of giving the service that they had planned to give. By contrast, the American students of limited means who shared the life of the Indian students could give and receive freely.

Next to wealth we must put *pride*. Here we come upon a complex psychological phenomenon, for we are thinking now not of the individual's proper pride, but of pride in a corporate body, corporate pride evinced of course very often in the conduct of an individual. The temptation to the wrong sort of pride in the Church to which one belongs is very subtle, because there is a right pride in one's church and in *the* Church. Anyone who has read any church history ought to be proud of the Church as well as ashamed of some passages in its history. But there is a corporate pride manifested by the Church that can do more than anything else to repel people from it and thus render it incapable of serving them. There is the sort of pride that insists on building a grandiose church on a strategic site, whether there are Christians there to fill it or not. There is the denominational pride of the Anglican who manages to convey by his vocabulary and manner that he considers Nonconformists beyond the pale. There is an historical pride, which concentrates exclusively on the glories and sufferings of my Church in the past, and ignores or forgets its failures and crimes. I once went into the porch of a parish church in Ireland and saw an interesting diagram of Irish church history. Under the year 1642 was written in large letters: 'Presbyterians Persecute the Church'. But I looked in vain against the year 1660 or later for any suggestion that the Church showed a considerable eagerness to persecute the Presbyterians. All this destroys even the possibility of the Church appearing as the Servant.

Thirdly, there is the *introvertedness* of the Church. This is a greater danger today than ever before. After all, the Church in most countries does not command the wealth it used to command, and the privileges and powers which it once possessed have been taken from it, so reducing its corporate conceit in many places. But it is increasingly conscious of being a minority under attack. In these circumstances the great temptation is to concentrate exclusively on its own life of worship and pastoral care of the faithful. In some countries in the world it is being driven to this position by a hostile government. And this is the last fortress to which it must retire under such conditions. The example of the Syrian Orthodox Church in Malabar, and of the Church in Russia since the Revolution, show that with within this fortress the life of the Church can be maintained for long periods. But it is not a situation which the Church should ever voluntarily embrace.

I remember listening with great interest once to an Irani Christian giving an account of his church. Quite casually he told us of the immense difficulties under which it existed: a tiny minority, associated with a foreign power in the minds of the people, facing a huge Moslem majority, it could only offer to those who joined it the certainty of opposition from their families and the likelihood of losing their jobs. I asked my Irani friend whether this did not make Christians in Iran very uncertain about the future of their church. 'Oh no,' he replied. 'We go on with our evangelistic efforts and our schools and hospitals. We know that the future is in God's hands.'

If a church in those circumstances can be outward looking, none of our churches in the West has any excuse for introvertedness.

6

THE CENTRE OF THE CHURCH

WHO FOUNDED the Church of Rome? The stock answer is: St Peter. But historical investigation shows that it is very unlikely that he founded it, though it is extremely likely that he ended his life in Rome. It is impossible to believe that Peter was in Rome when Paul wrote his letter to the Romans, as there is no hint in the letter that Paul was writing to a church where Peter was already at work. A very ancient tradition claims that the church was founded by Peter and Paul, but this again is contradicted by the evidence of the Epistle to the Romans. Paul was writing to a Church which he had not up to that point visited, and which was already a well-known and apparently flourishing community.

The truth is that we do not know who founded the Church in Rome; and this is in itself a very significant fact. What became the greatest church in Christendom was founded apparently not by any of the twelve apostles, or by anyone of whose activities we read in the New Testament. It probably just came into existence because there were Christians working in the metropolis of the Roman Empire. They naturally met for worship, and this constituted the Church in Rome. In other words, as far as the historical evidence goes, we can say that the Church in Rome began by being simply the Christians working at their daily business in Rome.

The Laity: the Church in the World

This brings us back to a fundamental truth about the Church

which has been overlaid by centuries of neglect. the Church at work in the world is the Christian doing his daily work in the world. This is forgotten equally by clergy and laity. Clergy forget it when they say of someone 'He is doing church work', meaning: 'He is in the direct employ of some one denomination with a head office in London'. And it is forgotten by the laity when they say of a man 'He went into the Church' meaning he is working as an ordained representative of the Church. Up to this point, when considering the Church's service in the world, we have confined ourselves to those activities which are officially undertaken in the name of the Church by the Church's appointed representatives, whether clerical or lay. We have discovered quite an impressive range of activities, but in fact, when we come to think of the life of the ordinary layman, we must see that these activities only cover a relatively small area of the actual service done by the Church. If you once begin to think of the Church at work in the world not just as clergy organizing laity to undertake some form of social service, but simply as the ordinary Christian at his daily work, the conception of the Church's service is immensely enlarged. The problems and difficulties also attending the Church's service in the world are quite different on this assumption. There is no point in asking in this context: how can the Church enter the world? The Church in all its members is already hard at work in the world every day. The question is much more: how can the ordinary Christian see his daily work as Christ's service of the world?

Obviously, it depends on the work. It is easy to see the work of a doctor as Christ's service but the work of a promoter of football pools is less concerned, if it is at all concerned, with the real service of mankind. It would be impossible to consider fully a question of this importance in a short book, but some guidance given by the New Delhi Assembly of the

World Council of Church in 1961 on the subject of political action reminds us of some important points. This is what they say about the Christian in politics:

(*a*) the Christian must remember always that he is by his action witnessing to Jesus Christ before men;

(*b*) at the same time, the Christian must always act in accordance with the particular local or historical situation in which he has been called to serve God and his fellow-men;

(*c*) the Christian must aways recognize that *Jesus Christ is the Lord of History and he is at work today in every nation of the world* in spite of and through the ambiguous political, economic or social structures and actions in any given country.

This statement suffers, as it was bound to do in the circumstances, from vagueness and generalization. But it does remind us of three essential things about this kind of Christian service.

First, it is *Christian* service. This must give us some sort of criterion for our daily work. To put it at its crudest: if by no stretch of the imagination you can honestly see your work as useful service to anyone, then you should not be doing it. This does not mean that you can turn valueless work into Christian service just by putting religious frills round it, like the advertisers who seek to redeem the ambiguity of their advertisements by inserting from time to time large posters saying: 'Come to Church!'

The second point made by the New Delhi Assembly throws great doubt over the value of those statements of 'Christian principles' that religious leaders so often produce when they are asked for guidance about the application of Christianity to daily life. Unless you know the circumstances, preferably from inside, you probably can't give very useful advice: a knowledge of Christian 'principles' without expert knowledge of the situation is no use.

The third point is perhaps the most important of all. In the last analysis, the service the Christian does is not his, but Christ's. Therefore he must not feel too keenly the burden of responsibility, because at the end of the day all he can say is: 'We are unprofitable servants'. This knowledge, far from inhibiting action, actually releases the Christian from that appalling feeling of responsibility that has driven so many high-minded humanists to despair, even to suicide: 'The fate of the world (or the nation or the community) depends on me!' Work done conscientiously by the Christian is his share in Christ's service; but it *is* Christ's service, and therefore the Christian need neither be proud because it has succeeded or overwhelmed because it has failed. The service of Christ is supremely expressed in the apparent failure of the cross.

In the last chapter we saw that the Church in its official capacity, organized in denominations, can supplement the work of the Welfare State. Probably the Church's most effective contribution to the service involved in the operation of the Welfare State lies in the Christian men and women who are employed in that service. This is a very hard thing for the clergy to accept. We clergy are still too much imbued with the notion that, properly speaking, we *are* the Church. The devout layman who cannot give direct service to the actual congregation with which he worships, because he is too much involved in his trade union, is often made to feel that he is failing the Church. I have met laymen who have obviously been ashamed that their work as doctors, or probation officers, or teachers has left them time only to worship on Sundays, and not to support church organizations and activities. The temptation of the parson is always to define Christian service in terms of direct help to the local congregation. 'How can the layman help the Church?' is the question asked. That sets us off on the wrong road from the start, for it assumed that the layman and the Church are somehow separate entities that have to be brought together. Then we say: 'There is plenty of work to be done: Mr A can take up the collection; Mrs B can lead the Mothers' Union; young C can address envelopes, and Miss D can play the piano.' We are back again at the old assumption that the Church essentially consists in the official organization centred in the clergy; whereas in fact it consists in the people of God, wherever they are.

I know of one Indian Christian layman who was in the Forestry Department of the Government of India. He was stationed as a Forest Guard in a remote village; and he caused a very great commotion in the village because he insisted on reporting to the police the names of those villagers who took timber in large quantities from the Government Reserve Forest without a licence. How, we may be asked, is this *Christian* service? He was only doing what a secular Government, made up of a great majority of non-Christians, was paying him to do. But that is just the point. That *is* Christ's service to the world, and Christians more than others ought to be concerned to see that such service is done loyally and with integrity. It is not that Christians have to think up strange things to do that would not occur to non-Christians. It is rather that Christians do the ordinary necessary jobs that have to be done, but do them for Christ's sake.

> A servant with this clause
>   Makes drudgery divine;
> Who sweeps a room as for thy laws
>   Makes that and the action fine.

I serve on the local committee of the Asia Christian Colleges Association in the town where I live. In our prospectus we say that our primary aim is to maintain the standard of education in the colleges of Asian countries. I have been challenged about this by earnest Christians: surely our first aim should be to convert people in Asia to Christianity? Yes, that is a task laid on us by Christ, but so is this other one; and the Church's service is not done merely as an aid to evangelism. Here is a case in point. I know very well a young Hindu doctor who in the whole of his medical training never had the chance to look through a microscope in the hospital laboratory, because he had not got the money to bribe the lab assistants to let him use one. Christian institutions are still needed to maintain high integrity and satisfactory academic standards. We do not run our hospitals and schools merely as a sort of bait for the Gospel. In fact if that was our aim, we should have to admit that we have failed. Christian service is an end in itself, and Christians would be bound to do it, even though no one should ever be brought to Christ by it.

The Church in the world today is much more like Joseph in Egypt than Moses in the wilderness. Joseph in Egypt served Pharaoh successfully because of what he had to contribute in the way of character and conduct; he served a king who did not acknowledge Jehovah, and we do not learn that any of the Egyptians were drawn to worship Jehovah as a result of his actions. Moses in the wilderness organized the entire life of the Israelites as a theocratic state. Nothing was done that could not be traced back to a specific command of the Lord. The situation of Moses in the wilderness corresponds to the situation of the Church in the Middle Ages. The situation of Joseph in Egypt (including the prison element) corresponds to the situation of the Church today. Nothing is to be gained by looking back with nostalgia to the Middle Ages, or by extolling the present period as the golden age of Christian liberty. We are to accept the sort of service possible to us as that which God wills for us; and we must believe that the situation in which the Church finds itself today is part of God's purpose. We can remember Pascal's admirable saying: 'The Church is in an excellent state when it is sustained by God alone.'

The Eucharist: the World in the Church

If the main impact of the Church's service is to be found in the lives of ordinary Christians carrying out their daily work, is there not a danger of Christianity becoming entirely secularised? Will the ordinary Christian not become immersed in the world? Have we not brought the laity into the centre of the picture only to exclude the clergy altogether? Not if the Christian's daily work is properly linked with worship. We did suggest at the beginning of this chapter that the Church in Rome at first consisted simply of Christians who had come to reside in Rome in the course of their business. But we added that they would naturally meet for worship on a Sunday. Now it is no coincidence that worship is called 'service' in ordinary speech. The service carried out in the world by the Church of the Servant and the service of Almighty God carried out by the worshipping Church are two sides of the one coin.

The New Testament gives us a plain lead here. In I Peter 2.5 the writer is addressing Christians:

> Like living stones, be yourselves built into a spiritual house, to be a holy priesthood, to offer spiritual sacrifices acceptable to God through Jesus Christ.

This sounds very unsecular language. It seems to bring the clergy properly into the picture; in fact it brings the priesthood in so emphatically that there doesn't seem to be any laity left! We are all priests, it seems, and we have 'spiritual sacrifices' to offer. These 'spiritual sacrifices' are not, however, to be thought of as exclusively abstract, as if the Christian was distinguished from adherents of other religions by the fact that his offerings were purely intellectual, or mental, or totally divorced from any external actions. In fact, when we look at St Paul's writings we find that these spiritual sacrifices are firmly tied down to the everyday world, to times and places, and visible objects. In Romans 12.1-2 he writes:

> I appeal to you therefore, brethren, by the mercies of God, to present your bodies as a living sacrifice, holy and acceptable to God, which is your spiritual worship. Do not be conformed to this world, but be transformed by the renewal of your mind, that you may prove what is the will of God, what is good and acceptable and perfect.

This RSV translation brings out Paul's meaning admirably. The presentation of our bodies is a living sacrifice, and is spiritual worship. In Paul's vocabulary 'bodies' here means 'complete personalities', so the Christian sacrifice turns out to be the offering of ourselves to God in Christ. Obviously this is not something that can be got over and done with on any one occasion; it is a life-long task. What is more, it is intimately connected with our daily work. In a profound sense, our work is the greatest part of our personality. It is after all what we exist to do—the reason for our being here rather than there. So the doing of our daily work acceptably to God is our offering, and is made in Christ. The Christian's service in his daily life is a large part of his offering to God and it constitutes perhaps the most important part of his spiritual sacrifice, the material on which he exercises his priesthood.

But it is also worship. How can we make sense of this? The daily life of the Christian *is* the Church's worship. What conceivable connection has this with what goes on in our churches on a Sunday? In very many churches today there is very little connection at all; but the early Church had no difficulty in seeing the connection and showing it forth. From what we can learn of their Sunday worship we find that they proclaimed the clearest link between work and worship, the service of our daily lives and the service of God in the Church's worship. For them the only service on a Sunday was the Eucharist, meaning 'Thanksgiving'. It was Eucharist at which every person present would normally receive the Holy Communion. If we briefly sketch out the shape which that service took, the connection between work and worship stands out.

1. *A Preliminary Section* in which the Word of God was set forth. This included readings from the Scriptures, a sermon, and intercessions for those in need.

2. *The Offering of the Bread and Wine* by the whole people. The actual way this was carried out differed in different areas, but in many places the deacons, representing the people, collected sufficient bread and wine from the congregation and brought it up to the celebrant, who was standing behind the table. The celebrant then formally offered the bread and wine to God as tokens and symbols of the offering of the whole people of God, their souls and bodies, their daily work. This was the spiritual sacrifice of the Christian priesthood.

3. *The Thanksgiving Prayer*. In a long prayer the celebrant gave thanks to God on behalf of the people for all his mighty acts in Christ. He would probably begin with the creation of the world through the Word, then certainly go on to mention the Incarnation, the institution of the Eucharist, Christ's death on the cross, and his resurrection, and the one offering which he made thereby on our behalf; and he would end by giving thanks that we are deemed worthy to stand before God and make this offering of thanksgiving. In this prayer the self-offering of the people of God was joined to the one great offering of Christ. What we do in our daily lives was publicly linked up with what Christ has done and still does, for us. Work, faith, and worship met and fell into their places in the one great whole.

4. *The Communion of the People*. All partook of both the bread and the wine. Here they believed they encountered the

living God, who used the tokens of their self-offering (the bread and wine) as the means by which he met them, accepted their offering in Christ, and sent them forth to the world again to carry on Christ's service there.

An act such as this does clearly show how the word 'service' can be used with equal justice of what Christians do in the world and of what they do in church. Worship is above all the service of God: we are bound to give him thanks for his mighty acts in Christ. But worship is also the service, the work of the Servant, in the world.

In the Eucharist the Church is consecrating the daily work of Christians. But the daily work of Christians is not normally different from the daily work of non-Christians. The general run of duties of a Christian mother, for example, are mostly the same as those of a non-Christian mother. The Church in the Eucharist is therefore in a sense consecrating *all* work to God. And this is an essentially priestly task. The New Testament does not speak of the clergy as priests, but it does use this word of the Church as a whole. The Church is a royal priesthood (I Peter 2.9). One important activity of that priesthood is the spiritual sacrifice, the bringing of the offering of oneself to God in Christ, and this has an essential place in the Eucharist. But there is implied here also another activity of that priesthood, the bringing of the whole world to God in Christ, and quite plainly it is the Church as a whole that must exercise the priesthood (not the clergy only, nor the laity only). In the Eucharist there is a place for this too: in that service we bring the world to God in Christ. Service in church and service out of church meet here.

To read any account of the worship of the early Church is to realize how appallingly far the Church today is from carrying out its prime duty; and how far the vast majority of Christians are from understanding the true connection between worship and life. In England on the whole, life seems to go on untouched by worship; and very often where the emphasis is on worship it is carried on by the clergy in such a way that it seems to have no connection with real life whatever. It seems a strange, technical sort of performance that has all the charm and unreality of a mediaeval mystery play. Here in Northern Ireland, where I am writing, worship is on the whole better attended (outside as well as inside the Roman Catholic Church), but it is not the service of the Eucharist that draws the people. The Eucharist has been pushed away to the periphery of the Church's life. It is an extra devotional exercise for the exceptionally pious. Or else it is the rare and solemn feat like the Jewish Passover, partaken by all but not more than four times a year. It is not, or not for more than a very few, the consecration of daily life, the window on the world, the meeting of the service of the world and service of God. An immense reformation in our ways of worship is due. I can only say that it has hardly touched Ireland as yet.

Conclusion

One should not say exactly 'the centre of the Church is the laity', for that would suggest a barren anti-clericalism. On the other hand for centuries we have all behaved as if the centre of the Church was the clergy, which is just as wrong. The centre of the Church is the ordinary Christian at his daily work: this is the Church's service *par excellence* and therefore the service of Christ the Servant. But in another sense the centre of the Church is the Eucharist. This is the place where all the Church's activities are brought to God in Christ. It is the service without which the daily service of the Christian would not make sense. Christianity is thus at one and the same time the most secular and the most priestly of religions, *secular* because the Christian's spiritual worship is carried out in his daily life, *priestly* because every Christian partakes in the great priestly act of eucharistic worship which the Church offers every Sunday.

But in the deepest sense of all, the centre of the Church is Christ. Hendrik Kraemer in a recent book has said that what is needed in the Church today is the clear demonstration that it is a Christocracy. Christocracy means that authority over the Church lies in the hands of Christ. We all admit that it does, but how are we to make this plain to the world? The largest denomination in Christendom is an autocracy, with the Bishop of Rome possessing all authority. Other large denominations (including my own) are organized as a democracy with the laity exercising extensive constitutional powers. These two methods of organizing the Church only illustrate the barren debate between clergy and laity for control of the Church. If I may be permitted to coin a new word, what we need in order to show forth Christocracy in the Church is not autocracy or democracy, but laocracy. *Laos* is New Testament Greek for 'the people', and what we need is the authority of the whole people of God.

7

THE EQUIPMENT OF GOD'S PEOPLE

IT IS the custom in the Roman Catholic Church on the Thursday in Holy Week to end the ceremonies with what is known as the Pedilavium. The bishop in his cathedral, or the abbot in his monastery, washes the feet of certain chosen persons. The ceremony is first attested round about AD 700. The giving of the Maundy Thursday money by the Queen is the relic of a similar rite; indeed it witnesses to the semi-sacerdotal character that the English sovereign once bore. A comparable ceremony of foot-washing is still practised in some denominations in America. All this is evidence that the Church as a whole has never completely failed to connect the work of the ministry with humble service. For all the authoritarian claims that have been made by the ministry at various times during the history of the Church, the feeling has always remained that ministers are there to serve. One of the Pope's official titles (first used by Gregory the Great about AD 600) is *Servus Servorum Dei*, Servant of the Servants of God.

In the theology of most Christians the conception of the ministry has included service. It has often been reduced to a mere formality by the other elements. But we have come to see the Church as bearing the form of a Servant; we have taken service to be not just *a* function of the Church, but its main, normative function. Must we not see the ministry in the same light? St Paul has shown us both that we cannot ignore the rôle of the ordained ministry in the New Testament and that it also is presented under the form of a servant. So the next question that arises is: how can the ordained ministry be a servant-ministry? How can the ministry also reflect the form of a servant? 'Ourselves as your slaves', said St Paul. The question is, how? In the light of the New Testament insight into the ministry of the Servant, can we say anything about the function or operation of that ministry?

Away from Hierarchy

The chief representative of the Church's ministry for by far the greater part of the Church's history and over the greater part of the world has been the bishop. If therefore the description 'servant' can be applied to the office of bishop, it can perhaps be applied to the Christian ministry in any circumstances. If what we have found in St Paul's letters about the ministry is a true picture, the bishop should be the servant of his flock, and in the long history of the office there is no doubt that there have been periods of history and areas of the Church in which this has been true. As we know the office in the West today, however, there are externals connected with the office which do not at all suggest that the bishop is primarily a servant.

Perhaps we can best put it this way: anything that seems to put the bishop on a lonely pedestal is dangerous. The task of the Servant-ministry is to be in the thick of the conflict: in I Corinthians 4 it is the Corinthians who have put themselves on a pedestal, and when the office of bishop first clearly emerges into history in the second century AD the bishop is one amongst his presbyters, related to them, to the deacons and to the people, not as the apex of a pyramid, but as one who has his special work to perform in the functioning of the whole church. The presbyters likewise have their work, the deacons theirs, and the people theirs. St Ignatius, for example, who was Bishop of Antioch in Syria and was martyred about AD 110, in one of his letters (Ephesians 4) compares the bishop to a lyre and the presbyters to the strings. God gives the note, and the individual members of the local church are to form themselves into a choir. This suggests a co-operative effort in which everyone has his special task to do, rather than a hierarchy with the bishop at the top and the layman at the foot of the ladder. Similarly in another letter Ignatius describes the whole Church in Smyrna as 'stewards, assessors and ministers of God' (Polycarp 6.1).

Is the very idea of 'hierarchy' at fault? Certainly in very early times the various orders in the ministry were not considered as arranged in a hierarchy. It was not necessary first to be a deacon, and then a priest, before one could be bishop. Instances can be quoted of men being ordained directly from the status of layman to that of bishop, without receiving the two orders of deacon and priest in between. Indeed, an exact hierarchy seems in practice to be more the effect of social circumstances than of anything inherently connected with the Christian ministry. It appeared in its most elaborate form in the Middle Ages in the West, when the feudal system greatly encouraged such a tendency. It is by analogy with the great feudal lords that the title 'Lord Bishop' derives and not from anything specifically related to the Gospel. Today it seems to import an undesirable social overtone to an office whose dignity does not need such an addition.

The idea of 'hierarchy' can appear in similar circumstances in churches which theoretically repudiate any inequality in the ministry at all. Bishop Michael Hollis, formerly Bishop in Madras, tells of an incident which took place shortly after the inauguration of the Church of South India in September 1947.[1]

Paternalism and the Church (Oxford, 1962), p. 47.

THE EQUIPMENT OF GOD'S PEOPLE

He was visiting a village in his diocese which up to the time of union had been Presbyterian. Theoretically, therefore, up to this time the Christians in that village should have known of nothing but one order in the ministry, with no scope for hierarchy at all. The village teacher, however, thought that he would have no difficulty in explaining to his flock the meaning of this new phenomenon, a bishop. The following dialogue took place between him and the villagers:

'You know that I am placed over you.'
'Yes.'
'You know that the district evangelist is placed over me.'
'Yes, he is.'
'You know that over the district evangelist is the local presbyter.'
'Yes.'
'And that over the local presbyter is the district missionary?'
'Yes.'
'Well, then, the bishop is simply the man who is placed over the district missionary. Now do you understand?'
'Why yes, of course.'

Those illiterate ex-Presbyterians did not need to be taught anything about the meaning of hierarchy: but we may suspect that the Indian social system had more to do with the formation of this particular hierarchy than had the demands of the Gospel.

God does not always leave it to us to mould the form of the ministry, or of the Church itself. He himself moulds it very often by what the Germans call 'his left hand'. That is, when the Church will not reform itself from within, God reforms it from without by the force of social, economic, and political circumstances. The insolent baron bishops of mediaeval Germany are superseded by Luther's Evangelical Church which dispenses with them altogether. The aristocratic prelate-bishops of the eighteenth century in England are reformed, regulated and partially disendowed by a Nonconformist-influenced government in the first half of the nineteenth century.

Perhaps God's left hand is pressing on the ministry in the West at this very moment. It is experiencing economic insecurity in an affluent society that has less and less use for full-time clergy. Is this God's way of reminding us of our servant status? It is always easier to see his hand in the past than in the present. At least this can be said: when the office of bishop is taken out of its Western 'Christendom' environment, and transplanted to a completely different social and economic environment in Asia, new aspects of the office (which are sometimes very old ones) can begin to appear. Take away the social position which the bishop undoubtedly has in the West, and, in some circumstances at least, the servant aspect appears more clearly. Here is an example of of this from my own experience.

In 1948-49 the part of Hyderabad State in South India where I was working was in a very much disturbed condition. Owing to political upheavals, various groups of bandits calling themselves Communists, with some genuine Communists among them, were able to terrorize the villagers in the remoter areas, and even attempted to set up a government of their own in some villages. The Indian government authorities responded by sending a special corps of armed police to patrol these areas, and one such police patrol was stationed in the small town which was the diocesan centre. For some reason the officer in charge was obsessed with the idea that the doctor in charge of our Christian hospital could give him valuable information about the local guerrillas, some of whom may have been his patients. This doctor, an Indian himself from farther south, had worked for over twenty years in that area: he was a Christian of great devotion and integrity, and had no more thought of aiding the Communists than the police officer himself. But he was summoned at intervals to the local police office and was put through a severe grilling. One afternoon an orderly from the police officer arrived at the doctor's house: he was wanted immediately at the police station. By this time the doctor was desperate and asked the bishop (an Irish missionary who had spent 35 years in India by that time, and spoke the local language extremely well) to go with him to try to establish his innocence.

Later we heard from the doctor and his wife what had happened. When they reached the police station the officer was in a very bad temper. He began by abusing the doctor and accusing him of complicity in all the outrages that had occurred in the neighbourhood. At this the bishop protested and said that the doctor was entirely innocent. The officer then lost his temper completely, turned on the bishop and began accusing him of being part of the conspiracy, using the foulest and most insulting language he knew. Through it all, the doctor told us, the bishop remained completely unmoved. He listened with a slight smile on his face as if he was being given a formal address by a welcome committee, and at the end he made not the smallest attempt to protest or retaliate. 'I have never in my life realized more vividly how far our bishop was prepared to go in sharing with us all our hardships and insults and dangers. That he, a man from another land, and a leader of the Church, should be prepared to accept abuse for my sake!'

Ministers and Ministry

The ordained ministry, as well as the Church as a whole, must show the form of the Servant. Whether this has any bearing on the ordering of the ministry is a question too large to tackle here. One might guess that in fact any form of ministry could show the Servant pattern of behaviour and could equally be so used as to obscure the Servant. Pastor, minister, bishop, Pope, are all capable of behaving as Servant, and all have on occasion 'tyrranised over those who were allotted to their care', to adopt the NEB translation of I Peter 5.3. The theology of the Servant does not give us definite guidance about the form of the ordained ministry. But it can illuminate the relation of the ordained ministry to the rest of the Church. This is a subject which has not received very much study in the history of the Church. A great deal of scholarship and research has been expended on discovering the lineage of the ministry, as also on proving that this or that form of the ministry is the right one. But few theologians seem to have stooped to ask: what is the relation of the ordained ministry to the Church? What is the ministry for? Above all, what is the connection between the ministry of the ordained minister (with which we are all so familiar) and the ministry of the Church as a whole (which is very often something that we have not thought about at all)?

Generally speaking, during the greater part of the Church's history one gains the impression that the ordained ministry has succeeded in establishing itself in a dominant position *vis à vis* the Church. We can trace, from at least the time of Cyprian onwards (died 258) a steadily growing tendency in the West to exalt the position of the clergy over against the laity. Perhaps the most dramatic manifestation of the dominance of clergy over laity occurred at Canossa in North Italy in 1077. The Emperor Henry I, the most exalted of the laity, stood in the snow for three days outside the lodging of Pope Gregory VII before he was granted absolution. And the most absolute proclamation of this dominance occurs in the Bull *Unam Sanctam* issued by Pope Boniface VIII in 1302. It contains these words:

> Furthermore we declare, state, define, and pronounce that it is altogether necessary to salvation for every human creature to be subject to the Roman pontiff.

On the other hand, by reaction from clerical dominance, the laity have sometimes succeeded in establishing themselves in a position of authority over the clergy, a state of affairs which is equally damaging to the true Servant character of both Church and clergy. The history of the Church of England since the Reformation too often gives instances of the State, often in the person of the Crown, wielding an authority which should properly belong to the Church as a whole; and we see clergy putting the interests of the State before those of the Church. Erastianism is no improvement on Ultramontanism. When we say that the ordained minister is a servant, we do not mean that he is a paid employee. Too often in the Free Churches the grim relationships between factory owner and factory worker which capitalism evolved have been introduced into the local church. How often have the deacons or the stewards reminded the minister whose views did not please them that he who pays the piper calls the tune?

It seems likely that one the greatest questions which the Church must face during the next generation is that of the relation of the clergy to the laity, or rather, the clergy to the Church as a whole. We have already (p. 59) quoted the New Testament passage which gives us the right picture. Here it is in full in the NEB:

He who descended is no other than he who ascended far above all heavens, so that he might fill the universe. And these were his gifts: some to be apostles, some prophets, some evangelists, some pastors and teachers to equip God's people for work in his service, to the building up of the body of Christ.

This makes it quite clear that the ordained ministry exists for the sake of the Church, and not *vice versa,* as much mediaeval thought and practice might suggest. The ordained ministry exists for the equipment of God's people as a whole for their ministry. In other words, the ordained ministry is given by Christ in order to equip all Christians to carry out their ministry in the world.

In fact, however, we clergy have succeeded very largely in reversing this relationship. We have managed to convey the impression to large numbers of ordinary Christian men and women that their main obligation as Christians is to 'help the Church'. And by 'the Church' we mean of course the functioning institution of which we are the centre. 'Won't you help the Church?' To ninety-nine out of every hundred of us those words are the prelude to a request for money or service for the purpose of maintaining the fabric of the Church or paying the clergy, or supporting some church activity designed to separate practising Christians from the rest of the world. We need nothing less than a revolution in our thinking here. We need to reverse the position and to teach the ordinary Christian in his daily life to think of himself as going about the work of the Church. We must not be satisfied till it is quite natural for him to approach his minister for advice or action with the request: 'Won't you help the Church . . . ?'

8

ONE WHO HAD AUTHORITY

'THEN THE Curate shall declare unto the people what Holy-days, or Fasting-days, are in the Week following to be observed. And then also (if occasion be) shall notice be given of Communion; and Briefs, Citations, and Excommunications read.' This is the rubric in which the Book of Common Prayer deals with what we would today call the notices or itnimations. It must be confessed, however, that among those notices an excommunication is rarely heard nowadays. When the Book of Common Prayer was composed there was still the remains of a system of church discipline operating in the Church of England. That system has now almost completely disappeared and has not been replaced by anything else. The same is true of the Free Churches.

In Defence of Excommunication

The reasons for this are two. First, the mediaeval system of discipline was grossly abused. Innocent people could incur excommunication for purely political reasons, and grave moral offences could be pardoned if sufficient pressure were brought to bear in the right quarters. But the second reason is even more obvious: the divided condition of the Church makes it impossible to enforce discipline. If a man were to be excommunicated by one denomination, he could simply transfer his custom to another, where he would probably be welcomed. A third cause might be found in the secularism of the West. Excommunication is no longer feared, and society as a whole in Western countries does not back it. It only remains effective in those countries, like Spain or Eire, where social or political circumstances have enabled the Roman Catholic Church to retain a commanding position. On the other hand, among the younger churches in Asia and Africa, church discipline is still a real force. Excommunication, or the threat of it, still has an effect on offenders. The Church is still able to enforce certain moral standards on its members by means of its disciplinary system. This is no doubt largely because there is still only one denomination at work in each area; the disunity of the Church does not therefore impair the Church's discipline. Also most of the denominations respect each others discipline, and will not accept excommunicated persons from other churches.

We can hardly deny that the Church ought to have authority to excommunicate offenders. Not only is it very plainly a right which the Church exercised in New Testament times, but, as we saw in chapter 4, our Lord himself claimed authority. The question therefore arises: how can the Church exercise authority and yet retain the form of servant? Can it, so to speak, combine the offices of servant and judge? Of handmaid and policeman? Here we must go back to the life of Jesus himself, and ask how he exercised authority. The authority of the Church stems directly from the authority of the Servant-Messiah, so his way of authority should show how the Church's authority is to be exercized.

In Mark 11.27 we read how the chief priests and the scribes and the elders challenged Jesus, and asked him:

By what authority are you doing these things, or who gave you this authority to do them?

Jesus answers by appealing to the authority of John the Baptist. He says in effect that his authority is the same as John's and if they can accept John's they ought not to challenge his. Now John's authority was not like that of the scribes, founded on an appeal to the written Law; nor was it like that of the priests, based on a succession going back to Aaron. It was essentially a prophetic authority; that is to say, it was self-authenticating. John simply claimed to speak for God, and those who heard him could judge for themselves whether his claim was true. Jesus means that his authority is like that also; it is self-authenticating. He did not rely on his Davidic lineage to gain him allegiance (Mark 12.35-37 makes this clear). Nor did he rely on the written Law to supply him with credentials.

What is even more significant is that Jesus even refused to give a 'sign' when he was asked for one. He says in Luke 11.29:

This generation is an evil generation; it seeks a sign, but no sign shall be given to it except the sign of Jonah.

The Scribes and Pharisees wanted something outside him that would authenticate him in their eyes, but Jesus refuses this. The only sign will be the sign of Jonah: the Ninevites, who were Gentiles, repented at the preaching of Jonah, and so will it be with the Gentiles in Jesus' day. His own people will reject him, and Gentiles will accept him. In effect, therefore, the sign that Jesus gave was the cross and resurrection and the spread of the Church. His authority was the authority of the crucified and risen Messiah, and sprang from nothing outside him. As Charles Wesley wrote:

I view the Lamb in his own light.

The application to the Church's situation is surely that the Church must not look to any outside agency to help it in enforcing its own discipline. For the first 300 years of its existence, this is the policy which the Church followed, and that was the age in which its discipline was most healthily exercised. Afterwards, when the Church became the favourite of the State instead of the target of the State's persecution, it became quite impossible to separate State-administered discipline and Church-administered discipline. In the West at least, the Church can hardly be blamed for this, for over large areas of the Western Roman Empire the State's machinery simply broke down, and any government there was remained in the hands of the Church. But even as early as St. Augustine's time (he died in 430), a Christian bishop spent a large part of his time sitting as a judge in a law court. The Reformation made very little difference to this as far as discipline was concerned. It was still assumed by everyone, Catholic and Protestant alike, that the State had a duty to enforce the Church's discipline. Only in the nineteenth century were the two forms of discipline finally separated. The Church became in effect a voluntary society, administering its own discipline as best it could, by voluntary means.

Our Lord asserted his own authority on his own authority and took the consequences, which were in fact the cross. The Church must today follow the example of its Lord, now it is left on its own once more. In the West, at least, these consequences would initially be in all probability unfair publicity and unpopularity, and, if similar situations in India give any guide, sentimental opposition from within. It was my experience that when in India some church member had committed some grave fault and showed no sign of either penitence or restitution, the question would inevitably come up: should not he (or she) be excommunicated? And almost invariably some apparently responsible person would argue against it on the grounds that such harshness was unchristian. God is love, after all, and he would not mean us to take a step that would cause so much distress, etc., etc. Indian Christians however, have no monopoly of this kind of sentimental misconception of Christianity; it is the current coin of popular journalism in Britain. We may be quite sure that if the Church did try to tighten its system of discipline and did pronounce sentence of excommunication on offenders, it would be considered a glorious opportunity by the popular press. The church authorities, whether bishops or presbyteries, would be characterised as narrow-minded Puritans, and foolish church members would write leters to the newspapers saying that after all it was the journalists who understood the real meaning of Christianity! No matter how obvious the breach of discipline, the offender would be portrayed in some popular newspapers as a martyr for freedom or for principle, and the church authorities as mediaeval bigots.

Authority in Teaching

The Church of the Servant must therefore exercise discipline. Serving the world does not mean condoning its sins. But Jesus not only opposed what was wrong in his day. He also taught with authority. We may ask: how can the Church teach with authority and still be the Church of the Servant? When we look at the Church as it is today, we find that its teaching authority is expressed through a very wide variety of methods. Indeed almost every denomination has its own peculiar method of promulgating the teaching which it wishes to be regarded as authorative. The Church of Rome, with its strongly centralised autocracy, tends to favour authoritative pronouncements by the Pope, which in some cases are claimed to be infallible. At lower levels, we encounter pronouncements by meetings of bishops or by individual bishops. The Anglican Church is tending nowadays to put most emphasis on the resolutions or advice of the Lambeth Conferences of bishops, though the decisions of groups of bishops in the various provinces of the Anglican Communion often carry much authority. But authority here is a relative affair, and even the most authoritative pronouncements are usually couched in an exhortative tone, as contrasted with the commanding note we find in pronouncements of the Roman Catholic Church. Other churches prefer resolutions of their supreme governing bodies as a means of conveying authoritative teaching; for example a resolution of the General Assembly of the Church of Scotland carries great authority in that church. In many churches, however, it is very rare to find any authoritative teaching issued in the name of the church. Sometimes there are no persons authorized to speak on behalf of the church as a whole, as appears to be true of the Baptists. Sometimes again the conception of the church as a whole speaking with authority seems to be absent.

As we look at these various methods of conveying authoritative teaching, it does not seem as if any of them was the ideal method for conveying the authority of the Servant. There is plenty of authority, for example, in the Roman Catholic system, but does it look like the peculiar authority of the Servant? It is Christ or Caesar speaking? On the other hand, it can hardly be right for the Church to abandon altogether the attempt to speak with authority. Perhaps there are two things, more than anything else, making it difficult for the world to see the authority of the Servant in the teaching of the Church. The first is arrogance. Too often the Church (in all its manifestations) has spoken with authority where it should have kept silence or said something different. We think of the Church's attempt to silence Galileo, of the Inquisition in the seventeenth century and of Bishop Wilberforce's attack on T. H. Huxley in the nineteenth. The second obstacle to the full manifestation of the authority of the Servant is undoubtedly disunity. The Church cannot speak with one voice. Perhaps the World Council of Churches is acting to some extent as a means by which this may be remedied. Certainly its pronouncements sound more like the voice of the Servant Church than do those of any one denomination. The consciousness of sin forced on the churches by the fact of their disunity is a healthy antidote to the pride which often accompanies the exercise of the Church's authority through one denomination.

How did Jesus show his authority? Not by making vast claims for himself, though such claims were implicit. His authority seemed to reside in what he was and what he did rather than in what he specifically claimed to be. Especially in Mark's gospel there is an elusive quality about his authority, the mystery of the hidden Messiah. His authority was at the same time most deeply hidden and most clearly expressed by his servanthood. We can only say the same thing about the authority of the Church of the Servant: the more the Church in its life shows forth the character of the Servant, the more will its teaching bear the marks of the authority of the Servant. Perhaps Origen (died 255) expressed the matter as well as anyone in his book against Celsus:

> Jesus is at all times assailed by false witnesses, and while wickedness remains in the world is ever exposed to accusation. And yet even now he continues silent before these things, but places his defence in the lives of his genuine disciples.

9

SERVICE AND MISSION

IT WOULD seem at first sight that the application of the Servant pattern to the *mission* of the Church ought to be fairly straightforward. In other spheres, such as that of the ministry or of worship, the evidence may be ambiguous or scanty, but we do have in the New Testament a clear picture of the Church actually carrying out its mission. All St Paul's letters were written in a missionary situation, and it was of himself and his fellow missionaries that Paul said to his Corinthian converts: 'We are your slaves for Christ's sake.' At the same time we can point today to a number of churches founded in Asia and Africa by the great missionary efforts of the last century, and we can witness to the continued interest and work for those churches among Christians in the West. May we not claim that in this at least the modern Church has not been unfaithful to the example of the early Church?

St Paul and the Missionaries

Unfortunately, however, the more closely we compare the missionary activity of Paul and his contemporaries with that of the churches of the West during the last century, the more we are aware of certain basic differences between Paul's situation and that of our Victorian ancestors. Paul certainly set out with a band of helpers to establish Christian churches all over the Near East and the Greek mainland. And he certainly claimed among the churches he established the authority of an apostle. He never hesitated to rebuke, direct, and exhort with the authority which he possessed from Christ. But at this point the resemblance to the modern missionary movement ceases.

Paul was a member of a race which was considered inferior by most Greeks and Romans. He had, it is true, Roman citizenship, but that did not save him from a great many undignified, humiliating, and painful experiences, as both the Book of Acts and his own writings testify. He came from a part of the Roman Empire that was economically poor, and, far from disposing of large sums of money to be spent on his converts, he seems to have had no capital, but to have relied to a large extent on supporting himself by his own labours during his missionary tours. One of his first aims once he has founded a new church is to induce it to contribute to his fund for poor Christians in Judaea. Moreover, he did not bring with him a richer culture than that which his converts enjoyed. One can, of course, exaggerate the Greek character of Paul's converts. It seems likely that most of his converts came, not from pure Greeks or pure Jews, but from members of mixed race, people who would have a fairly shallow culture anyway. But it is plain from passages such as Acts 17 and I Corinthians 2.1-5 that Paul's message had to meet the charge of being barbarous and unphilosophical. In a sense therefore we can understand the superiority complex of the Corinthians depicted in I Corinthians 4.6-13. Paul and his helpers must have looked quite like servants as they delivered their message against the background of the Graeco-Oriental civilization in which they lived.

The situation in which the nineteenth-century missionary movement began was quite different. Most of the missionaries were inspired by St Paul's example, and the churches which they founded were much closer to the New Testament Church than to the churches from which they had themselves come. But neither their own background nor their relation to their converts was in the least like Paul's. The great majority of them came under the protection of an imperial power maintained by men of their own race. It is neither a mere coincidence nor a disgrace that the missionary movement followed the Eastward expansion of the Western nations. The British at least made strenuous efforts not to use their power in India deliberately for the advancement of missionary work, but it was too much to expect the illiterate peasant to distinguish between the authority of the District Collector and the authority of the District Missionary. Again, the missionary came from a civilization that was economically far in advance of that in the midst of which he worked. In fact, he was part and parcel of that immense influx of Western ideas and techniques which is transforming both Asia and Africa (today, now that independence has arrived, even more rapidly than before). It was quite impossible that he should not be identified in the minds of Indians, whether Christian or not, with Western methods, Western money, and Western education. Finally, up till recently the missionary unconsciously assumed that he represented a superior culture. In the case of Africa, this was true. In the case of Asia, it was an arrogant illusion. But it meant that the Western missionary arrived in Asia with a confidence in himself which did not all derive from his faith in the Gospel.

Problems in Asia and Africa

The consequence has been that the Church of the Servant, whatever its intentions, has not on the whole borne the image of a Servant in its missionary activity. It is true that countless missionaries have in fact given deeply sacrificial service to Asia and Africa, but the missionary on the whole has not appeared in the guise of a servant to those among whom he has worked. Still less have the sending churches in the West given the impression of being servants and handmaids of the churches they

SERVICE AND MISSION 117

have founded in the East. On the contrary, up till recently the churches in both Asia and Africa have been missionary dominated. Indigenous leadership has been slow to appear, and political dependence on Western rulers has been matched by ecclesiastical dependence on Western churches. Spontaneous expansion, original thought, local initiative have all been much too rare. With political independence church autonomy has now been established almost everywhere. But economic dependence is still very far from being removed. The number of churches in Asia and Africa which could continue without Western subventions to maintain the institutional life of their Church at the present level must be extremely small—if indeed any such exist outside China.

There is another element in the situation with which St Paul and his fellows did not have to contend: disunity. The missionary movement of the last century did not found one Church overseas, but dozens. It is unnecessary here to underline the evils of disunity in a non-Christian environment, but it must be pointed out that disunity prolongs dependence on the West. If the Church in Asia and Africa is to operate as a number of independent organizations, each linked up with a world denomination, it cannot make full use of such resources as it possesses in order to make itself truly autonomous. It cannot stand on its own feet if its first loyalty is to Rome, or Canterbury, or New York, and not just to the totality of Christians in its own country, the people of God in Ceylon, or Bengal, or Nigeria. As I write, certain Anglicans in England are striving to discourage their fellow Anglicans in North India from going forward to union with their fellow-Christians in North India on the ground that they would be infringing Catholic principles; and certain Presbyterians in Ulster are doing the same thing to their fellow-Presbyterians in North India on the ground that they would be abandoning Reformation principles. Each party would like to use the weapon of economic sanction to enforce its views on the Church in North India. Each would evidently like to keep their respective denominations in North India still under their own thumb.

The whole relationship between the sending church and the receiving church is vitiated by these historical circumstances. It is extremely difficult for the West to be constantly sending out missionaries to the churches in Asia and Africa without unconsciously dominating the life of these churches. With the best will in the world, we Western Christians sometimes find it difficult genuinely to respect the freedom of the churches overseas. To take an example from my own Communion: in three vast areas of Africa recently the Anglican Church has attained full autonomy. We now have a Province of West Africa, a Province of East Africa, and a Province of Uganda. But our mission secretaries and other experts in the United Kingdom and United States still talk about 'missionary strategy for the Anglican Communion'. If this phrase means anything, it can only mean church leaders in the West planning the evangelistic programme of churches in the East. This is not the work of a servant, but a master. It may be, as suggested above, that the very existence of our world-wide denominations, with their headquarters inevitably fixed in the West, makes it virtually impossible for the mission of the Church to become the mission of the Servant.

The truth is that if you are a source of free monetary aid, it is extremely difficult to maintain the rôle of a servant. Quite apart from the fact that the ownership of money inevitably means the possession of power, money creates vested interests and sub-Christian legal relationships. I know of one area in India where a mission is maintained by the devoted efforts of supporters in the West. The Church in that area is very small, under five thousand in all; but in the past the missionary society has built up a whole series of institutions, schools, a hospital, and a college. The original intention was that they should serve the purpose of evangelism as well as of social service, but today the second object has entirely eclipsed the first. The institutions are doing splendid work serving the community. But the small Christian Church in the area cannot ever hope to keep these institutions going, either in funds or in staff. The result is that the Church there has not developed as it should in responsibility, whether you look for indigenous leadership or self-support. The sending church, as represented by the Western missionary society, has failed to present the form of a servant. It appears more like a development corporation.

Towards an Eastern Church

What is to be done in order to bring the missionary efforts of the Western Church today more into the pattern of the Servant? The first thing is that Western Christians should be informed about what has happened. Here we encounter a genuine difficulty: there is so much to give thanks for in the life and witness of the churches in Asia and Africa that it seems ungrateful to point out the deficiencies in their life. Again, they have undoubtedly much to teach us, and one does not want to put anything in the way of Christians in the West learning from their brothers and sisters in the East. Also, it would be foolish and indeed criminal suddenly to cut off all supplies of money and missionaries on the grounds that the churches overseas must be self-dependent at once. One usually finds that the leaders of the missionary activities of the Western churches are fairly well aware of the position, and are anxious to encourage indigenous leadership and self-support. But still there is a great work to be done among the ordinary church-going public in the West. The public image of the missionary, of the missionary society, and of the church overseas has to be changed. From my own experience I know that the ordinary man in the pew and the ordinary man in the pulpit believe that the Church in India and Africa should be, and is, exactly like his own church, only attended by men of different colour. This belief has to be radically altered.

Secondly, we can be more ready to accept God's 'left hand'. This has already happened in China. It is far too early to estimate how exactly the Church in China has developed since 1950, but it is by no means certain that the removal of all missionary and financial support has been an unmitigated disaster. Obviously a similar development may take place in other parts of Asia and Africa. We should not eagerly expect this, but we can sometimes anticipate it. In some places the Church in the West can best carry out its mission as the Servant by doing all it can to ensure that the Church in the East can if need be dispense with its services.

Thirdly, churches in the West must learn to look at their own denominations through the eyes of Christians in the East. The Servant Lord so identified himself with us that he did in actual fact look through our eyes. To us, our denomination is a source of pride: we feel an intimate link with our fellow church member in Fiji, and we think how wonderful it is that we belong to a communion which spans the entire globe. We do not normally reflect that this sense of solidarity is very often gained at the expense of the unity which we ought to be experiencing with our fellow-Christian next door, who belongs to a different denomination. Such a pan-denominational solidarity is a luxury which members of the relatively small churches in Asia and Africa simply cannot afford. We Western Christians at the moment are asking them in effect to forego the experience of union with their fellow-Christians in their own country in order that they may continue to experience our idea of solidarity with the world-denomination to which they happen to belong. But such an experience is not for their real good, not at least if it is made a substitute for local union. Membership of a world-denomination means at the moment in effect accepting Western leadership, Western initiative, Western methods. All our world denominations, including the Church of Rome, cannot but be Western dominated. We maintain them as independent denominations at the cost of the indigenous, autonomous Eastern Church of the future.

We must encourage, rather than discourage, local unions in Asia and Africa. We tend at present to discourage them in effect, while often praising them in principle. Often the churches in the East are trained to be too dependent on our opinion, too anxious to have full approval of their actions, even when formally independent churches. They see that union with their fellow Christians in their own country is necessary if they are to survive, but union is going to be such a shock, it is going to require such mental adjustments, make such demands for original thought, deprive them so often of precedents to solve their difficulties in advance. And we in the West often dislike the idea of the very name of our denomination disappearing. What, no more Anglicans in India? No more Methodists in Nigeria? It hurts our denominational *amour propre*.

But the ultimate aim the Church mission has before it is to do the work of the Servant. If we encourage our churches in Asia and Africa to enter local unions, we may see some strange and unprecedented forms of church life. But we will not ultimately be disappointed. We shall find that out of the death of the denomination springs the life of the Catholic Church. A death is an essential part of the mission of him

who did not come to be served, but to serve, and to surrender his life as a ransom for many.

Appendix

DEACONS

IT MAY well seem strange that nothing has been said about the order of deacons in the Church. After all, the very name means 'servant', and one might naturally expect that the origin of the office would be connected with the servant quality of the ordained ministry. Unfortunately, however, the order of deacons is something about which the Church has never apparently been able to make up its mind.

The very origin of the office is obscure. Most modern scholars believe that the 'Seven', whose appointment in Acts 6 is traditionally taken as the institution of the office, were not deacons in any sense at all. Luke never describes them as deacons. He uses the word *diakonein* of what they are to do, but, as we have seen, this is a word with a wide extension in the New Testament. Nor do they do anything that is associated with the later deacon, such as helping with the liturgy or administering church funds. Paul seems to refer to deacons once, in Philippians 1.1, but I would contend that the word means nothing more specific here than 'church workers'. It is in the Pastoral Epistles (almost certainly not by Paul) that we first find clear reference to the order of deacons, but we do not learn much about what the deacon was to do. Indeed, the list of qualifications for the offices does not differ much from those for the office of presbyter-bishop.

In the Church of the second and third centuries, the diaconate does emerge as a specific office. The two main tasks we have mentioned already. The deacon had a special rôle in the

Eucharist, acting as a sort of mediator between celebrant and people. And he did administer church funds under the bishop. Indeed he seems to have had a special relationship to the bishop; it was not at all unusual for a deacon to succeed the bishop whom he had been serving, without being ordained to the presbyterate in between, e.g. Athanasius in 328.

In later times, both in East and West, the diaconate degenerated into a probationer stage for the priesthood, and this is what it appears to be throughout 'catholic' Christendom today. Thus the third order in the threefold ministry is nothing very much more than a fossilized remnant. At the Reformation the various reformed churches made efforts to restore the primitive diaconate, but none of them can be said to have succeeded: the Church of England left the mediaeval arrangement untouched. In some parts of the Reformed Church the diaconate still appears as a tenuous office, always held by a layman, connected with finance and church property. In the Congregationalist and Baptist churches the word 'deacon' is used to denote what would be called the 'elder' in the Reformed churches.

In fact, the diaconate is still awaiting revival and rediscovery on the part of the Church. The order of deacon does not therefore throw any light on our investigation, except in so far as its history suggests that the Church may have intended to concentrate in this office the servant element in the ordained ministry's vocation, and then forgot about the original meaning of the office.

FOR FURTHER READING

C. R. North, *The Suffering Servant in Deutero-Isaiah* (Oxford University Press, 2nd ed., 1956). By far the most informative book in English, though rather inconclusive. Professor North's simpler exposition of *Isaiah 40–55* is in the Torch Bible Commentaries (SCM Press, London, and Macmillan, New York).

H. W. Robinson, *The Cross in the Old Testament* (cheap ed., SCM Press, 1961; USA: Westminster Press), contains a powerful meditation on 'The Cross of the Servant'.

T. W. Manson, *The Servant Messiah*: A Study in the Public Life of Jesus (Cambridge University Press, 1953).

W. Zimmerli and J. Jeremias, *The Servant of God* (Eng. tr., SCM Press, 1957; USA: Allenson). This is the article on the word 'servant' by two German authorities in the famous *Theologische Wörterbuch z. N.T.*, edited by Kittel.

Aage Bentzen, *King and Messiah* (Eng. tr., Lutterworth Press, 1955). Many of his conclusions would be disputed, but the book is interesting as representing the contribution of a Scandinaivan scholar.

M. D. Hooker, *Jesus and the Servant* (SPCK, 1959). Dr Hooker surprised the learned world by denying that Jesus ever thought of himself as Servant in the sense of Isaiah 53, defending her point with great competence. I think that she will prove to have made some good points, but not her main one.

H. H. Rowley, *The Servant of the Lord and Other Essays* (Lutterworth Press, 1952). A balanced estimate of the biblical evidence by the leading authority on the O.T. in England.

R. H. Fuller, *The Mission and Achievement of Jesus* (SCM Press, 1954). An account of the significance of our Lord by one who knows his Bultmann well without being a disciple.

Lewis S. Mudge, *In His Service* (Westminster Press, Philadelphia, and St Andrew Press, Edinburgh, 1959). A study of 'The Servant Lord and His Servant People' by the Theological Secretary of the World Presbyterian Alliance, which has given special emphasis to this theme. Dr Mudge has a more technical study of Servant Christology in preparation for the SCM Press.

Hendrik Kraemer, *The Theology of the Laity* (Lutterworth Press, 1958; USA: Westminster Press) is a summary of the teaching of the former Director of the Ecumenical Institute about the biblical basis of the revolution needed in our thinking about 'church life'.

INDEX OF BIBLICAL REFERENCES

OLD TESTAMENT

Genesis		*Isaiah (continued)*		*Isaiah (continued)*	
26.24	12	20.3	25	50.4-9	19, 21
42.13	11	28.9	25	52.7	29, 30, 42
		35.9	32	52.13-53.12	19, 22-24
Exodus		40.1	14	52.13	44
3.12	12	40.9	29-30	53.1	42
32.32	25	41.8-10	15	53.3	33
		42.1-4	19, 20	53.5	32
Numbers		42.1	37	53.10	22
12.6-8	12	42.6	31	53.11	36
		42.18-19	16	53.12	32, 33, 39, 57
Deuteronomy		42.22	13	55.3-5	17
30.14	41	43.8	16	60.6	30
		43.10-12	16	61.1	30
II Kings		43.19-21	17		
8.13	12	44.1-2	15	*Jeremiah*	
		44.7-8	17-18	11.19	25
Psalms		44.8	17		
78.70-71	12	44.24-26	17	*Joel*	
116.10-19	52-53	45.23	41	2.32	41-2
116.16	12	48.6	17		
		49.1-6	19-21	*Amos*	
Isaiah		49.3	44	3.7	13
5.1-7	38	49.24-25	33		

NEW TESTAMENT

Matthew		*Mark (continued)*		*Mark (continued)*	
16.17-19	65-66	9.12	33	14.21	35
23.10-12	34	9.30-31	35	14.24	30
23.35	36	10.18	57	14.27	35
28.16-20	66	10.32-34	35	14.36	37
		10.38	35	14.49	35
Mark		10.43-45	31, 32, 34, 121		
1.11	37	11.27-28	108	*Luke*	
1.14-15	29, 30	12.1-11	38	4.17-18	30
1.22	67	12.35-37	109	4.21	38
8.27-9.1	65	13.32	28	11.21-22	33

INDEX

Mark (continued)		Romans (continued)		II Corinthians (continued)	
11.29	109	10.14	42	12.19-13.10	62
12.50	35	10.15	42		
13.32-34	35	10.16	42	Galatians	
14.7-11	34	10.17	42	4.26	53
17.7-10	57-58	12.1-2	93		
22.25-27	34, 47	15.7-12	40-41	Ephesians	
22.27	32, 33			4.1-11	59
22.37	32	I Corinthians		4.9-12	105
		1.10-17	46	4.11-14	59
John		1.25	49		
3.14	44	2.1-5	115	Philippians	
8.28	44	3.18-4.13	46-50	1.1	63, 122
12.32-34	44	4.6-13	115	2.1-11	41
13.1	44	4.12	56	2.6-7	39, 40
13.12-16	67	4.15	61	2.7	59
13.31-32	44	4.21	62		
14.13	44	7.10	62	I Thessalonians	
15.8	44	7.25	62	5.12-13	63
18.37	37	7.40	62		
20.19-23	66	11.2	62	Hebrews	
		11.17	62	2.5-18	41
Acts		11.23	51	11.37	25
8.34	24	16.15-16	63	13.17	63
15.6	64				
15.22	64	II Corinthians		I Peter	
20.17-38	64	2.1-9	62-63	2.5	92
		4.1-15	50-54	2.9	95
Romans		4.13	57	5.1-5	63
4.1	55	5.14-6.10	54-59	5.1	63
10.8	41	5.20	49	5.3	47, 104
10.13	41	10.5-6	62		

INDEX OF NAMES

Aeschylus, 18
Agamemnon, 19
Anglicanism, 61, 111
Antigone, 18
Asia Christian Colleges Assoc., 90
Athanasius, 123
Augustine, 110

Babylon, 14
Baptist Church, 123
Basil of Caesarea, 123
Boniface VIII, 104
Book of Common Prayer, 107

Canossa, 104
Church of England, 79, 80, 105
Church of Ireland, 71, 84
Church of Rome, 61, 78, 86, 98, 108, 112, 121
Church of Scotland, 112
Congregationalist Church, 123
Cyril of Alexandria, 28
Cyprian, 73, 104
Cyrus, 14

Deenabandhupuram, 77

Eire, 75-108
Eliot, T. S., 19-20
Euripides, 18

Free Churches, 61, 105

Galileo, 112
Gladstone, 71
Gregory the Great, 98

Gregory VII, 104

Henry I, 104
Hollis, Bp. M., 100
Huxley T. H., 112
Hyderabad, 71, 102

Ignatius of Antioch, 99, 100
India, 75, 116
India, Republic of, 72
India, South, 11, 71
Iran, 85

Kerala, 75
Kraemer, H., 97

Lambeth Conferences, 111

Manson, T. W., 61
Maundy Thursday, 98

New Delhi Assembly, 87
Nigeria, 75

Origen, 112

Pascal, 91
Pedilavium, 98

Sophocles, 18
Syrian Orthodox Church, 85

Wesley, Charles, 109
Wilberforce, Bp. S., 112
World Council of Churches, 112

www.ingramcontent.com/pod-product-compliance
Lightning Source LLC
Chambersburg PA
CBHW050836160426
43192CB00011B/2054